Paragraph

A Journal of Modern Literary Theory

Volume 31, Number 1, March 2008

Roland Barthes Retroactively: Reading the Collège de France Lectures

Edited by Jürgen Pieters and Kris Pint

Contents

An Unexpected Return: Barthes's Lectures at the Collège de France JÜRGEN PIETERS AND KRIS PINT	1
Atonality and Tonality: Musical Analogies in Roland Barthes's Lectures at the Collège de France LUCY O'MEARA	9
'The *Paideia* of the Greeks': On the Methodology of Roland Barthes's *Comment vivre ensemble* MAARTEN DE POURCQ	23
How to Become What One Is: Roland Barthes's Final Fantasy KRIS PINT	38
'Except When Night Falls': Together and Alone in Barthes's *Comment vivre ensemble* DIANA KNIGHT	50
Suspending Events, Loving the Margin: Solitude According to Barthes SABINE HILLEN	61
Barthes without Althusser: A Different Style of Marxism JEAN-JACQUES LECERCLE	72

The 'Inkredible' Roland Barthes NEIL BADMINGTON	84
'*Préparation du romanesque*' in Roland Barthes's Reading of *Sarrasine* ANDY STAFFORD	95
Preparing the Novel: Spiralling Back JONATHAN CULLER	109
Notes on Contributors	121

An Unexpected Return: Barthes's Lectures at the Collège de France

JÜRGEN PIETERS AND KRIS PINT

'I undertake therefore to let myself be borne on by the force of any living life, forgetfulness. (...) Now comes perhaps the age of another experience: that of *unlearning*, of yielding to the unforeseeable change which forgetting imposes on the sedimentation of the knowledges, cultures, and beliefs we have traversed.' (*IL*, 478)[1] With this promise to deliver himself to the forces of forgetfulness, Roland Barthes concluded his inaugural lecture on 7 January 1977, when he joined the Collège de France as professor of literary semiology. He would teach there for three years, until he was hit by a laundry van while crossing the street — a traffic accident that would lead to his death a month later, on 26 March 1980.

It is rather ironic that while Barthes's writings continue to be read and taught as the work of one of the pioneers of more than one critical school in modern literary theory, this teaching of 'unlearning', this exploration of the forces of amnesia in his lecture courses at the Collège de France, was almost forgotten for more than two decades. Although his inaugural lecture was already published in 1978, it was not until 2002 that Barthes's notes of the first two *Cours* appeared, entitled *Comment vivre ensemble (1976–1977)* (how to live together) and *Le Neutre (1977–1978)* (the neutral). The series was completed with the publication in 2003 of *La Préparation du roman (1978–1980)* (the preparation of the novel), consisting of the notes of the last years Barthes lectured at the *Collège*.[2] In 2005 the first English translation of the courses appeared: *The Neutral*, translated by Rosalind Krauss and Denis Hollier; translations of the other two lecture courses, by Richard Howard, are on their way.

For Barthes-aficionados, these lecture courses may be somewhat disappointing, at least at a first reading. In terms of content, the notes are surely not the most exciting part of Barthes's work. They were never intended to be published, and therefore they often lack the intensity of books like *S/Z* and *A Lover's Discourse*, two books that were based on lecture notes Barthes rewrote before publication.

Barthes's hesitation to make a book out of his courses at the *Collège* has partially to do with fundamental doubts about the direction these lecture courses should take. Barthes had exchanged the closed, intimate atmosphere of his seminars at the École pratique des hautes études for a crowded, anonymous auditorium in one of France's most prestigious academic institutions. The transition was intimidating, especially because it coincided with the illness and death of his mother, with whom he had lived together for most of his life. Barthes's mourning, heartrendingly expressed in *Camera Lucida*, also profoundly marked his lecture courses. They often seemed to lack the vitality, the versatility of his earlier work. As Jonathan Culler confesses in his contribution to this issue, the courses were at times so dull that he frequently skipped classes.

But Barthes's doubts were not only caused by his private situation – they also revealed a theoretical uncertainty that had haunted his work ever since he detached himself from the existentialist, Marxist and structuralist systems of thought, to find himself unprotected, 'in the open', as he called it in *Roland Barthes by Roland Barthes*.[3] In *The Pleasure of the Text* and *A Lover's Discourse*, Barthes emphasized the importance of the desiring and enjoying body of the individual reader, who deliberately allows himself to be lured into the imaginary of classic texts and to be carried away by the affects and the *pathos* these texts evoke. At the same time, Barthes was looking for a way to use this *pathos* as the basic principle of what he called in his inaugural lecture an 'active semiology', a semiology which

collects the impurity of language, the waste of linguistics, the immediate corruption of the message: nothing less than the desires, the fears, the appearances, the intimidations, the advances, the blandishments, the protests, the excuses, the aggressions, the various kinds of music out of which active language is made. (*IL*, 470–1)

The ideal semiologist for Barthes is therefore no longer a detached, even prudish scientist, but a Nietzschean artist, personally involved in the language he examines:

He plays with signs as with a conscious decoy, whose fascination he savors and wants to make others savor and understand. The sign—at least the sign he sees—is always immediate, subject to the kind of evidence that leaps to the eyes, like a trigger of the imagination, which is why this semiology (...) is not a hermeneutics. (475)

No longer interested in the development of a rigid methodology, Barthes preferred artistic principles to explore those 'various kinds of music' of language. In her contribution to the present volume, Lucy O'Meara shows how atonal music, with its stress on incompleteness and coincidence, provided the rationale for Barthes' active semiology. The first two lecture courses consist of a collection of 'traits', short, independent fragments, presented as pieces of a jigsaw puzzle the listener has to put together. Even with the help of the audio-recordings of the courses, which are available in MP3 format, Barthes's notes are not easy to read. They are jotted down in an elliptic style, with short phrases often only connected by logical symbols ($=, \neq, :, \rightarrow$), and hence demand an active participation of the reader to be understood. Together, these 'traits' create a *writerly* text, an 'open work' where 'interpretation' should be understood rather as performing a musical score than elucidating a meaning. Eventually however, this 'atonal analogy' becomes less evident for Barthes. This is especially the case in the last two lecture courses which together form *La Préparation du roman*. In these courses, Barthes not only admitted his growing preference for classical literature, but also for classical – tonal – music. This evolution had a noticeable affect on the construction of the courses. They become more structured and more 'developmental', as we follow Barthes in his untimely quest to blend the old and the new and his — unsuccessful — efforts to conceive a literary counterpart of 'a work in C major' in the age of post-serial music.

This desire for the untimely is also recognized by Maarten De Pourcq as a decisive factor in Barthes's interest in classical antiquity. In the first lecture course of *Comment vivre ensemble*, Barthes introduced the Greek notion of *paideia* as a valuable pedagogical alternative for the rigidly methodological approach he rejected in his active semiology. By retracing the original context of the notion of *paideia*, De Pourcq points out that Barthes's use of this notion is far from historically accurate. In fact, Barthes's specific appropriation of the term is a perfect illustration of how he sees this *paideia*: the collection of different fragments of cultural knowledge from the most disperse areas, without much care for the original context or meaning. Or as Barthes puts it in *The Neutral*: 'I try to create, to invent a meaning from independent materials, which I liberate from their historical, doctrinal "truth" $\rightarrow$ I take the referential bits (in fact, bits of reading), and I submit them to an anamorphosis: a process known to all mannerist artists.' (*N*, 65) Together, these fragments or 'traits' make up the different entries of a idiosyncratic encyclopedia or 'enkyklios paideia', referring to a kind of 'general education' that is no longer legitimized by an external, objective truth, but by the subjective desire which these fragments arouse in the reader–compiler.

In his contribution, Kris Pint examines how Barthes tries to conceptualize this relation between knowledge and desire, between body and text, by using the psychoanalytical notion of *fantasy*, to which Barthes gave a Nietzschean–Deleuzian twist. As he already announced in his inaugural lecture, each lecture course takes a personal fantasy as its starting point, functioning as the connection between the various 'traits'. By following these fantasies as a compass needle, Barthes sets out for a new style of living, a *vita nuova* in which life is turned into a work of art. It is this Nietzschean ideal of the artist-philosopher that inspires the ethical question underlying each lecture course: 'How to live?'

But this question immediately implies a necessary supplement: 'how to live *together*?' How is this personal desire expressed in the fantasy to be reconciled with the desire of others? This fundamental problem plays a crucial role in the central fantasy of *Comment vivre ensemble*, the desire for a utopian community that would find the right balance 'between solitude and encounter' (*CVE*, 101) by adopting the guiding principle of 'idiorrythmics'. Barthes discovered this notion — by chance — in a book about Greek monks on Mount Athos, who live a solitary, secluded life, with occasional gatherings and celebrations. This single word 'idiorrythmics' suddenly activated within him a fantasy of living-together and opened it into a 'field of knowledge' (*CVE*, 38) in which he could wander freely, discussing literary and philosophical texts in order to elucidate certain aspects of this fantasy.

One of the most important intertexts in *Comment vivre ensemble* is Thomas Mann's *The Magic Mountain*. As Diana Knight notes in her contribution to this special issue, the remote sanatorium where Hans Castorp lived for seven years functions as a secular equivalent of the monastery on Mount Athos. Knight relates this intertext to Barthes's own experiences as a TB-patient in a 'sanatorial society' and discusses how his ambiguous feelings towards such an enclosed way of living became a recurrent theme in Barthes's work, long before he identified the underlying fantasy in his lecture courses. In her discussion of *Comment vivre ensemble*, Sabine Hillen points out how this problem of living-together eventually boils down to a problem of language. Any use of language is characterized by some kind of violent repression, as our personal rhythm cannot but be disturbed by the 'rhetorical rhythm' of the other — in his inaugural lecture Barthes even hyperbolically stated that language itself was 'quite simply fascist' (461). But without language, without communication, no community would be possible. It is this problem, so crucial to the notion of idiorrhythmics, that leads Barthes to the subsequent fantasy of the neutral, which inspired his second lecture course. The desire for the neutral is defined by Barthes as an active desire for everything that 'outplays' and 'baffles' the paradigm (*N*, 6), for that which cannot be reduced to a fixed term in the set of binary differences which — as we have known since Saussure — structure the language system. The neutral, if only for a moment, jams the infernal machine of language and affirms the meaningless, scarcely noticeable nuance. As Barthes makes clear, this neutral position is almost impossible to achieve. Even the use of adjectives, an essential class of words, inevitably implies a violation of the delicate principle of the neutral. By attributing an adjective, be it depreciatory or meant as a compliment, I force the other into a paradigm, burden him or her with a set of expectations, while imposing my own values. In his essay, Jean-Jacques Lecercle points out the similarities and differences between Barthes's critique of language in *The Neutral* and Althusser's notion of interpellation. But although there remains indeed an important 'Marxist substratum' in these lecture courses, Marxism as a critical discourse is kept at bay. Since for Barthes ideology is not *expressed* in language, but almost *coincides* with it, the discourse of Marxism itself cannot but share the same arrogant characteristics of the ideology it claims to criticize. Instead, Barthes tries to conceive a non-arrogant theory of language. As Neil Badmington argues in his contribution, this theory is based on the materiality of writing, in the most literal sense. By lingering over his own writing habits and preferences for certain colours of ink and certain pens, Barthes's focus on the writing process meticulously 'denaturalizes' the meaning produced by the text. We could call this a materialism of the detail, which is inspired much less by Marx than by Nietzsche. Or as Barthes puts it in *La Préparation du roman*, to defend his seemingly exaggerated attention to the specific writing habits and tricks of famous writers: 'All this trivial? Dragged in? — I always look at this from the perspective of Nietzsche's *Ecce Homo*: the postulation of a profound *Philosophy* connected to apparently insignificant choices: the choices of the body.' (*PR*, 307–8, italics in the original)

Eventually Barthes came to the conclusion that only the act of writing, and in particular the writing of literature, allowed one to catch a glimpse of the Neutral. Consequently, the fantasy of the Neutral gave way to another fantasy, the desire to write a novel: 'In relation to our notion of the Neutral, I would say: the Novel is a discourse without arrogance, it does not intimidate me; it is a discourse which does not exert pressure on me – hence the desire to attain myself a style of discourse which does not exert pressure on others.' (*PR*, 41) This fantasy would occupy Barthes for the next two lecture courses, *De la vie à l'œuvre* and *L'Œuvre comme Volonté*, which together constitute *La Préparation du roman*. In these courses, Barthes discussed the many choices and problems a would-be writer encounters in his pursuit of the desired object, the Novel, and especially the problem of finding the right style. As such, *La Préparation* in fact reflects on Barthes's own evolution towards a more essayistic, even literary way of writing. Andy Stafford traces this fascination for the novelistic, the 'romanesque' back to *S/Z*, where Barthes performs a slowed-down, 'drugged' reading of Balzac's short story 'Sarrasine', which provokes in the reader a loss of self. As such, the passive reception of a literary work is turned into a productive 'writerly' act that runs off with the outlined identity of both the literary character and the reader. This way of reading deconstructs the classic narrative structure of the novel, but saves the novelistic style. In *S/Z*, the writerly text is thus defined by Barthes as 'the novelistic without the novel'.[4]

In *La Préparation du roman*, however, Barthes tries to reconcile the 'novelistic' style with the classic genre of the Novel. This return to the Novel goes hand in hand with another unexpected return, the return of the author. In his notes, Barthes confesses to a growing 'biographic curiosity' for the authors he admired, and advocates a 'dé-refoulement' (de-repression) of the author (*PR*, 276), whose figure was branded by Barthes as the sworn enemy of the 'writerly' at the time of *S/Z*. In the later years of his life, the private life of authors like Proust and Kafka became a source of inspiration, as they succeeded in transforming their life into literature, in turning themselves into a literary character and thus realized the *vita nuova* to which Barthes himself aspired. In the final essay of this issue, Jonathan Culler points out that this return to the author is not the only surprising twist in *La Préparation du roman*. In his last two lecture courses Barthes also pleaded for the undervalued aesthetics of the readerly and lamented the indifference of young writers towards their own writing, as they no longer sacralized it as an Oeuvre, a *magnum opus*. With his critical assessment of these lecture courses, Culler in fact reveals the tragic dimension of Barthes's teaching at the Collège de France. Barthes really wanted to become a Nietzschean 'artist-philosopher', capable of the great *Umwertung aller Werte* (transvaluation of values) and of forgetting all those 'knowledges, cultures and beliefs' that formed the intellectual *doxa* of his day, only to discover that he could not radically do away with them. Barthes was used to going against the grain, but now he found himself in the uneasy situation whereby the theoretical *doxa* he opposed was to a great extent influenced by his own thinking. So when, in *La Préparation du roman*, he vehemently denounced the smug contempt of contemporary literary theory for biographical issues, Barthes was well aware that *he* was one of those responsible for this anathema on the author in the first place. The lecture courses therefore offer the fascinating, if disconcerting view of a man shadowboxing with an earlier self, whose points of view were, as Culler argues, often far more convincing. It is indeed true that Barthes's 'active semiology' continuously runs the risk of becoming an ally to those reactionary theoretical positions he had so fiercely criticized in the past. Yet Barthes tried to make these outdated positions return on another, *higher* place on the spiral, to use one of his favourite expressions, of literary theory. He hoped that a revision could open unforeseen possibilities for semiology, even if this revision often turned into a mere regression, 'a spiraling back' as Culler puts it. The lecture courses themselves offer no solution, as the desired Novel which could express the Neutral and as such create an idiorrhythmic discourse, remained unwritten. But by following his fantasies, even if this sometimes led to naive, untenable fallacies, Barthes valorized Lacan's dictum that 'the non-duped err'[5]. By no longer falling back on theoretical claims, be they existentialist, structuralist or Marxist, these lecture courses disclose to us with hindsight the personal obsessions which had inspired Barthes in the past. If they teach us one thing, it is that to affirm one's recurrent 'bêtise' (stupidity) is perhaps a necessary condition for thinking and writing creatively in the first place. And by leaving the riddle of his desire unsolved, with no Novel to fill in the empty slot, this desire is passed on to us, his readers. These lecture courses should therefore not be considered as a final post-scriptum to his oeuvre, after which the files on Barthes can be closed. On the contrary, they are an invitation to return to his oeuvre and to explore retroactively the future possibilities for literary theory they perhaps still contain. And more importantly, they are an invitation to discover and explore our own fantasies as researchers along the way.

We should therefore read, or rather, re-read Barthes, according to his own definition of semiology in the inaugural lecture, as

that journey which lands us in a country free by default; angels and dragons are no longer there to defend it. Our gaze can fall, not without perversity, upon certain old and lovely things, whose signified is abstract, out of date. It is a moment at once decadent and prophetic, a moment of gentle apocalypse, a historical moment of the greatest possible pleasure. (*IL*, 476)

Enjoy the change of scenery.

NOTES

1 Roland Barthes, 'Inaugural Lecture, Collège de France' in *A Barthes Reader*, edited by Susan Sontag (New York, Hill and Wang, 1982), 457–78. Page references follow the abbreviation *IL* and are included in the text.
2 Roland Barthes, *Comment vivre ensemble. Simulations romanesques de quelques espaces quotidiens*, edited by Claude Coste (Paris, Seuil/IMEC, 2002) (page references follow the abbreviation *CVE* and are included in the text; translations are our own), *Le Neutre*, edited by Thomas Clerc (Paris, Seuil/IMEC, 2002) and translated as *The Neutral* by Rosalind E. Krauss and Denis Hollier (New York, Columbia University Press, 2005 (page references follow the abbreviation *N*), and *La Préparation du roman I & II*, edited by Nathalie Léger (Paris, Seuil/IMEC, 2003) (page references follow the abbreviation *PR*; translations are our own).
3 See Roland Barthes, *Roland Barthes by Roland Barthes*, translated by Richard Howard (Berkeley, University of California Press, 1977), 102 (translation slightly modified).
4 Roland Barthes, *S/Z*, translated by Richard Miller (New York, Hill and Wang, 1974), 6.
5 See Lacan's 1973–74 seminar with the same name (the title in French, 'Les non-dupes errent' is also a pun on the Lacanian notion of 'les noms du Père').

Atonality and Tonality: Musical Analogies in Roland Barthes's Lectures at the Collège de France

LUCY O'MEARA

Abstract:
Though explicit references to music are infrequent in Barthes's Collège de France lectures, Barthes's use of music in other work from the 1970s makes it clear that music can act as a fruitful analogy in consideration of the text. This article uses the serialist or atonal analogy, as set up by Barthes in 'From Work to Text' and elsewhere, to examine the structuring of *Comment vivre ensemble* and *The Neutral*. In viewing these courses as serial or open works we can, it is hoped, arrive at a fuller understanding of their methodology and the role they ascribe to the listener or reader. The atonal analogy, however, is left behind in 1978, as Barthes's major projects (*La Préparation du roman* and *Camera Lucida*) employ more conventional, developmental structuring. It is here, then, that the analogy with tonality, again suggested by Barthes, can be usefully employed.

Keywords: Barthes, methodology, Umberto Eco, open work, atonality, tonality

The majority of Barthes's texts on music date from the last decade of his life. For Barthes the mythologist and semiologist, music remains absent from critique, inviolable and uninstrumentalizable.[1] Barthes is determined to consider music as being exempt from the (ideological) meanings that literature is 'condemned' to. There is certainly a sense in which Barthes makes what Johan Fornäs calls the 'romanticist mistake' of seeing music, semantic and not semiotic, as the great other of text.[2] Characteristically, however, Barthes is aware of the dualism. His essays on music advocate a shifting of 'the fringe of contact between music and language'.[3] Music should force us to conceptualize our writing differently, in other words. It is useful as a *metaphor*: that, perhaps, is its preeminent merit for the writer, as Barthes concludes in 1978: 'Perhaps a thing is valid only by its metaphoric power; perhaps that is the value of music, then: to be a good metaphor.'[4]

Barthes's essays on music frequently involve a summation which posits music as the tutelary metaphor par excellence in terms of consideration of the workings of textual meaning. 'Rasch' (1975), for example, concludes with an offset line of text reading 'By music we better understand Text as *signifiance*'.[5] This, as Peter Dayan has pointed out, is a fairly standard instance of a certain Pater-esque modernism which uses the non-representational art of music as 'the founding metaphor of art in general'.[6] However, it is in writing that is *not* overtly concerned with music that Barthes bears out the promise hinted at so frequently in the essays on music. In work on the theory of the text he provides musical analogies which elucidate his concerns regarding avant-garde textual structure and how this implicitly assigns a certain role to the reader. Classic readerly structure, Barthes points out in *S/Z*, is similar to tonality, in that it encourages a reading as circumscribed and conditioned as the way we listen to the melody and harmony of classical music: 'one might say there is a *readerly eye* as there is a tonal ear', writes Barthes, and both of these involve strictly limited scope for interpretation (*S/Z*, 30, italics in original, translation slightly modified).[7] Atonality and serialism, in contradistinction, lead to the liberation of listening, and, by extension, of reading—hence their aptness in figuring the textual experience. Barthes expands the analogy in the essay 'From Work to Text' (1971) when he suggests that the reading of the text—as opposed to the comparatively passive consumption of the work—requires of the reader a collaborative production of meaning. We must *play* the text:

> [T]he reader (...) *plays at* the Text (ludic meaning), he seeks a practice which reproduces it; but, so that this practice is not reduced to a passive, interior *mimesis* (the Text being precisely what resists this reduction), he *plays* the Text; we must not forget that *play* is also a musical term. (*FWT*, 62–3, italics in original)[8]

He points out that 'the history of music (as practice, not as "art")' is 'parallel' to the history of the Text: for both fields, it used to be the case that 'active amateurs [were] numerous', and that ' "to play", and "to listen" constituted a virtually undifferentiated activity' (63). This equivalence mutated over time, however, says Barthes, such that we are now a society of '(passive) amateur[s] who listen to music without being able to play it'. In reading, the comparable problem is that reading has been 'reduc[ed] to consumption', which has robbed us of our active reading ability to such an extent that we merely feel ' "boredom" (...) in the presence of the modern ("unreadable") text' (63).

Active reading is vanishing because current methods of teaching reading forget that learning to write is an important factor in awakening the faculties required for engaged reading. This is a problem that looms large in Barthes's penultimate lecture at the Collège de France in 1980, when he discusses the problems attendant upon the writer's 'separation' from sociality. Ten years previously, the writings on Text indicate the importance for Barthes of the *amateur* (in music and in reading): a liberated society, according to Barthes, would recognize the importance — the vitality — of amateurism.[9] He seeks to free active reading from its confinement to the intellectual and professorial 'caste', demonstrating that we can learn our way back into the recognition and desire for active reading via the analogy with post-serial music:

We know that today post-serial music has disrupted the role of the 'interpreter', who is asked to be in a sense the co-author of the score which he completes rather than 'expresses'. The Text is a little like a score of this new kind: it solicits from the reader a practical collaboration. (*FWT*, 63)

The experience of post-serial music, in other words, is vital in helping us to work out what the polysemous, open Text requires of us, and what, in the shape of conditioned, passive reading, we must now leave behind. Atonality or serialism is the perfect analogy, because this music demands that the listener pay full attention to each instant of the music as it occurs. A complacent listening, facilitated by the knowledge that resolution according to a coded series of tonal progressions is never far off, is not possible for a serial work as it is for tonal composition. The sequences of twelve-tone and serial music are free of any gravitational pull toward or away from a tonic homeland. In the absence of any possible reliance on prefabricated blocks of tonal material, post-Schoenbergian music has to become stringent, atomized, unpredictable — especially in view of its concerted use of aleatory techniques.

This emphasis on chance and the instant, and the concomitant disorganization of the structural and experiential 'time' of the work constitutes, precisely, the use-value of the atonal analogy for Barthes's writing and teaching. In the *Préparation du roman* lectures, during his discussion of the idea of a *critique pathétique* which would focus on 'moments of truth' (*PR*, 160)[10], Barthes refers several times to contemporary music in order to illustrate his points. In the lecture on Proust that was in part redelivered as the first lecture of the *Préparation du roman* series, Barthes states that the innovation of *In Search of Lost Time* inheres in the manner in which it is based 'on a provocative principle: the *disorganization* of Time (of chronology)'.[11]

This point is elaborated by quotations from Nietzsche and John Cage: 'Nietzsche (...) says that "we must reduce the universe to crumbs, lose respect for the whole" and John Cage, prophesying the new musical work, announces: "In any case, the whole will constitute a disorganization."'[12] This use of Cage to support the valorization of temporal disorganization or rupture in Proust is very much in line with the manner in which, in *La Préparation du roman*, Barthes refers to Webern and Cage when discussing short, fragmentary forms: their music is the metaphor for the ideal condensation of (literary) form: 'The privileged art of the instant is music, sound = the *eidos* of the instant (Cage's theories).' (*PR*, 85)

The atonal analogy is far more fundamental to Barthes's work, however, than this localized use of Cage implies. We can see the quintessence of post-serial music — its focus on the instant, its aleatoriness and sense of incompletion — as being central to Barthes's concerns in his last decade. The vertical, fragmented structures of his book-length texts from this period bear witness to this. When Barthes insists on the particular use-value of the experience of serial and post-serial music, he figures the reader's role in collaborating with this sort of text. But it is in the Collège de France *Cours* that the openness, the 'serialism' of Barthes's late work is most apparent, having, as it does, an important pedagogical goal. The atonal analogy, I would argue, can be comprehensively applied to these lectures, and gives us the means to construct an understanding, not only of what our experience of the *Cours* is expected to be, but also of their methodology, and the rationale underpinning their constitutive incompletion.[13]

Open works, according to Umberto Eco, inaugurate an important shift in our experience of art. The poetics of an open work 'sets in motion a new cycle of relations between the artist and his audience, a new mechanics of aesthetic perception, a different status for the artistic product in contemporary society', states Eco. 'In short, it installs a new relationship between the *contemplation* and the *utilization* of a work of art.'(*OW*, 22–23, italics in original)[14] Every participant in the artistic experience, in other words, is afforded the opportunity for involvement and expression of a sort. As Pierre Boulez, another practitioner and theorist of the open work, puts it, the work develops 'an ethical [as well as an] aesthetic category'.[15] Ethicality, for Eco and Boulez as for Barthes, lies in the possibility for active participation in the artwork and its restoration of our critical faculties. It is the inclusion of this possibility that motivates the structure of the lecture courses *Comment vivre ensemble* (1977) and *The Neutral* (1977–78).[16]

The *Comment vivre ensemble* lectures were written during the same period in which the fragments of *A Lover's Discourse* were being prepared for publication.[17] The preface to *A Lover's Discourse*, entitled 'How this book is made', uses musical metaphors to illustrate the serialist manner of the book's construction and to justify the disorganized method of reading which this construction encourages. Barthes writes that the 'figures' of the text are 'no more than a modest supplement' offered to the reader; that ideally the book 'would be a co-operative: "To the United Readers and Lovers"' (5). The figures themselves 'explode, vibrate (...) like a sound severed from any tune — or (...) like the motif of a hovering music' (7). They have no narrative order or hierarchy, and are arranged aleatorically. The construction of the *Comment vivre ensemble* lectures is identical to this. The 'figures' are now called 'traits'. As in the *Lover's Discourse*, the traits are subjected to the 'arbitrary' classifications of nomination (each figure is assigned a name) and subsequent alphabetical ordering. He employs this aleatory principle, he says, in the aim of 'break[ing] the fixedness of language and draw[ing] closer to our own fundamental discontinuity' (*CVE*, 52). While the fragmentation of discourse may be only a small step in this direction — 'a false, or impure, or attenuated discontinuity' — it is worthwhile nonetheless, as Barthes feels that by this means he can guard against the vaguely-figured pernicious effects of a continuity in discourse which does not reflect lived experience. His position in this regard is reminiscent of the way in which Adorno and Eco, in their writings on music, attack tonality for its promotion of 'psychic inertia' in the listener because of its predictable linearity (*OW*, 80).[18] Barthes is anxious that the 'traits' should not group themselves into themes:

For me (...), every thematic grouping of *traits* unfailingly gives rise to the question (...) why this, why that? (...) = my reflex is to mistrust associative ideology (which is an ideology of development). The card-player's motto: 'I cut the deck', I act against the fixedness of language. (*CVE*, 52, italics in original)

Barthes also indicates, early in the Collège de France teaching, that he feels that a certain humility, rooted in a non-exhaustive knowledge of the subject under discussion, is necessary for a productive pedagogical relationship. The manner of the lectures' construction will mean that the pertinence of the material may not always be forcefully apparent — because 'this is research which is forming itself. I really believe that in order for the teaching relationship to work, the speaker must know only a little more than the listener (or even, on some subjects, less). (...) This is research [a search: *recherche*], not a lecture.' (*CVE*, 52)

These two determining factors as set out in the 'Présentation' of *Comment vivre ensemble*—the rupturing of continuity and the renunciation of mastery over the material presented—correspond to features of the open work as identified by Eco. Even more striking are Barthes's frequent exhortations that the listeners use the material he presents them with (the thinness of which he often apologizes for) to produce their own ideas and investigations. As he puts it in the course summary written retrospectively for the Collège yearbook, 'The research has consisted of "opening dossiers", with the listeners left to fill these dossiers according to their fancy. The teacher's role was mainly to suggest certain articulations of the theme.' (*CVE*, 221) Throughout the lecture series, Barthes constantly reminds his listeners of how he figures their and his respective roles: 'The lecture course (its traits) = a chequerboard of squares (...). I begin by setting out the squares and by more-or-less filling them. But it goes without saying that the squares can be filled by other people.' (*CVE*, 57) The commendation of the material to the listeners' care bespeaks an interesting array of concerns: that this education should indeed constitute a *leading out*; that the executive control of teacher and researcher be considered secondary to the additional avenues of inquiry which they may lead to in other minds; that the listener bears a certain responsibility and is expected to enter, at the very least, into active reflection on the material presented.

This complex of issues, comprised, it seems, of both renunciation and expectation on the part of the 'author', becomes clear when, at the end of the lecture series, Barthes describes at some length the manner in which the lectures have been structured. This 'protocol of exposition' uses various metaphors to figure himself as the presenter of open materials. 'I set out the squares (...) It's up to everybody to fill them in: a game for several people: a jigsaw puzzle. I'm the artisan who cuts out the wood. You are the players.' (*CVE*, 181) He also describes the course as resembling a pointillist painting, wherein the colours are juxtaposed on the canvas, and not mixed on the palette. 'I juxtapose the figures in the classroom, instead of mixing them at my own desk. The difference is that there is no final painting: the best thing would be for you to paint it.' (181) From this perfect statement of the theory of the open work, Barthes goes on to rearticulate his own humility, or his distancing of himself from his material:

> The exposition of a figure isn't exhaustive. I'd go even further (this is maybe a way to acquit myself (*m'innocenter*))—ideally, the lecture course would be one

where the teacher — the speaker — would be more banal than his listeners, and so what he says would be in the background of what he awakens [in others]. (...) If the course is a symphony of propositions, the proposition has to be incomplete. Otherwise it's a position. (180)

Barthes sees his 'protocol' as being constitutively incomplete — 'It is a preparation whose completion is endlessly postponed.' (183) There is no end-product, apart from the possibilities that are offered to the listener. Barthes makes it clear that this open method, and the mode of experience which it brings about ('we don't know where it's going'), is the central preoccupation of his teaching. In the final *Comment vivre ensemble* lecture, he refers to the following year's course:

What [will the] subject [be]? I don't know yet. What I have just said about non-method makes it clear that, ultimately, the 'subject' (*quaestio*) is not important. Whatever I choose as a 'subject', the digressive practice, the right to digression, will be exercised. I will always be saying the same thing. Indirectness will be used, and that is an ethical question. It will concern an *ethics*. (184)

The manner of the material's treatment is of more importance than the material itself. The construction is 'ethical' because of its expectation that the listener will be awakened by it to responsible interpretation. Limited as this action may be, action, rather than passive contemplation, is the outcome. To paraphrase Eco, the lectures' 'precise pedagogical function' lies precisely in their 'continual violation of patterns and schemes', a violation which seeks to return autonomy to the listener 'at the level of both perception and intelligence' (*OW*, 83); to make of him, in fact, an *amateur*.

The Neutral, as promised, 'says the same thing' as *Comment vivre ensemble* in its method, perhaps even more insistently. Once again, the 'figures' are treated aleatorically. The course takes the pedagogical ideal of *Comment vivre ensemble* a step further, in including listeners' comments and suggestions as 'supplements' within the lectures themselves. In this way, says Barthes, 'the Course = a process of collective memory: (...) this type of dialogue equally excludes praise and aggression but achieves an activity' (*N*, 136). Once again, also, the 'figures' are described as encouraging personal divagations from the source material. The 'sequence of fragments', Barthes states in the first *Neutral* lecture, puts into operation a state of 'continuous flux (*variation continue*)', which is articulated without any intimation or encouragement of 'a final meaning.' This system is similar 'to contemporary music, where the "contents" of forms matter less than their circulation.' The mode of construction determines that the fragments, perforce, become points of departure for the listeners: 'Each figure: as if one were establishing a bridgehead: after that everybody is free to scatter in the countryside: his own countryside. Accepted principle of nonexhaustivity: to create a projective space.' (N, 10)

Barthes remarks during the same lecture that the difficulties inherent to his use of aleatory construction tend to be overlooked by commentators:

> It's fine to (...) discuss the concept of fragment, it's fine to have a theory of the fragment — I am regularly interviewed about it — but no one realizes what a problem it is to decide in what order to put them. There is the real problem of the fragment. For me, still in the stage of infancy: 'electronic' chance = solution. (12)

The question of how to order his material, imbricated as it is for Barthes with ethical and pedagogical issues, is also technically challenging. This placing of the 'problem of the fragment' before the audience is one of the most obvious examples in the *Cours* of Barthes making the audience privy to the difficulties inherent to the construction of the work at hand. Indeed, as we have seen, one of the most insistent topoi in *Comment vivre ensemble* and *The Neutral* — so insistent, in fact, that it can be seen as providing the sort of thematic unity that the material itself so vigorously denies — is Barthes's foregrounding of his methodology. As the final statement of *Comment vivre ensemble* indicates, the method becomes the matter, and that will be the 'same thing' which Barthes will reiterate from year to year: the task of 'making it new' is passed from the teacher to his listeners, and the pedagogical hierarchy as well as the process of creative enquiry is problematized. To use the terms employed by the musical semiologist Jean-Jacques Nattiez, the *poietic* dimension (the problems and processes of creation) and the *esthesic* dimension (the restructuring that the 'receiver' performs 'in the course of an active perceptual process'[19]) become inextricable:

> The goal of the artist, as with Mallarmé, is to transmute this esthesic clash [i.e. interpretive activity, plurality] into a normative poietic principle: *normative*, since the openness of the work is perceived as a value that should be realized, and *poietic* because the perceptive indeterminacy is going to be transferred to production.[20]

Comment vivre ensemble and *The Neutral*, in their foregrounding of *poiesis* and *esthesis*, and in the way in which the concern regarding the esthesic pole actually dictates the *poiesis*, can thus be seen as 'open works', the theory of which Eco derives from contemporary music.

Moreover, their status as pedagogical material means that they *carry out* the liberatory pedagogical promise which Eco sees as being potentially present in the open artwork. This is another way of saying, as Thomas Clerc does in his preface to *The Neutral*, that the 'course' begins to resemble a 'work'. (*N*, xxiii)

In *La Préparation du roman* the inextricability of poietic from esthesic preoccupations is perhaps even more evident: both series of the *Préparation* are, after all, intensely concerned with rendering the difficulties of *poiesis* apparent to the listener. Barthes, arguably, goes as far as it is possible to go in the foregrounding of the act of creation, which, interspersed as it is with frequent references to the audience and their potential perception of this 'narrative', is manifestly concerned with the perceptual response framing the lectures.[21] The poietic and esthesic poles collide as the *Préparation* exhaustively discusses the desire to write and the difficulties encountered in the attempt to bring this desire to fruition. In Nattiez's terms, then, the *Préparation* could be an open work, as the would-be writer's poietic difficulties are handed over to the audience. However, its structure renders this problematic. The *Préparation* is rigorously sequential and developmental. Its second series is overtly structured like a play or a book, as Barthes says: it has an epigraph, an argument, three main 'chapters', and it concludes with a 'suspension'.[22] This work is, in other words, tonal: atonal or serial construction has been left behind.[23] Moreover, the end of the *Préparation* formulates the postulated work, towards which the entire series has been pointing, as also being resolutely tonal. Coming as it does in the context of Barthes's discussion of the 'trial of separation' suffered by literature, the writer, and the lover of literature, the use of music here constitutes the metaphorical locus of Barthes's sense of his being 'separated' or out of time: the music invoked, therefore, must be 'untimely' too.

As we have seen, Barthes has recognized the use-value of the atonal analogy and espoused the historical necessity of 'the tremendous break in tonality which modernity ha[s] produced'.[24] This recognition involves, perforce, a coterminous admission that works employing classical harmony which predate the advent of serialism are now out of date. And, of course, they are the objects of Barthes's love and emotional investment, as post-serial music never is. All of Barthes's texts on music have at their heart his repeated assertion that the Romantic music which he loves, and thereby he himself as its advocate, is untimely. The most succinct formulation of this comes at the conclusion of 'Loving Schumann' (1979), an article contemporaneous with the writing of the *Préparation* and strikingly similar in expression and preoccupation to the end of those lectures:

Loving Schumann (...) is in a way to assume a philosophy of Nostalgia, or, to adopt a Nietzschean word, of Untimeliness. (...) Loving Schumann, doing so in a certain fashion *against* the age (...), can only be a responsible way of loving: it inevitably leads the subject who does so and says so to posit himself in his time according to the injunctions of his desire and not according to those of his sociality. But that is another story, whose narrative would exceed the limits of music.[25]

This placing of himself against his era, and the suggestion that this emplacement is relevant to other spheres beyond that of music, is precisely what we have at the end of the *Préparation*, when Barthes describes the writer as suffering a triple separation. His love of literature separates him from sociality, from history and from language. The writer's being out of time is the tragedy which he must assume as his burden. One must reconcile oneself to this, he writes, and valorize this separation. Barthes goes on to give an outline of the 'Work' which the reconciled writer — he, or somebody else — could write, 'so that reading it would give me the same overwhelming emotion as certain works from the past. (...) The desired work must be *simple, filial, desirable*.' (PR, 378, italics in original)

Having outlined the qualities of the desired work, Barthes concludes by explaining why he cannot now produce this work. It may be, he says, because of 'a certain moral embarrassment' due to his consciousness that his attention is fixed on works of the past: 'my Desire reaches out toward forms which ignore so much contemporary work: this is something difficult to assume, or something you're sure you must assume' (384). Again we are reminded of the close of 'Loving Schumann'. Then, the entire final paragraph of Barthes's last lecture is couched in musical terms. A new work might be possible, writes Barthes, if a new way of *listening* could come about:

Doubtless the New Work (...) will not be possible (...) unless an ancient taste is transformed and a new taste appears. So perhaps what I'm waiting for is a transformation of [our] Listening — and maybe this will come to me, without metaphor, through music, which I love so much. (...) Thereby, the dinstiction between the New and the Old would be quite naturally done away with; the path of the spiral would be followed, and Schoenberg's words would be honoured. For it was Schoenberg, who founded contemporary music and rechannelled ancient music, who said this: it is still possible to write music in C major. That, ultimately, is the object of my desire: *to write a work in C major*. (384, italics in original)

Atonality and Tonality 19

If Barthes's oft-used spiral figure is a temporal unfurling, then we see that its trajectory here is conceived such that 'contemporary music' or atonality is subsumed into a narrative whose endpoint is placed beyond it, in an imagined time which resolves the old and the new musics. Tonality *returns*, and we are left with the desired work in C major, the simplest key, the key of white notes. But the work does not exist. Barthes tells us, earlier in the final lecture, that the desired work, 'simple, filial, desirable', is 'a white Work, the Degree Zero of the Work (an empty square, but one that's been extremely significant in the system of my life)' (378). 'A work in C major', as the final words of Barthes's last lecture, function in the same way as the closing phrase of his first book, *Writing Degree Zero*: 'the Utopia of language'.[26]

The work in C major is postulated as utopian, perhaps a sort of *anterior* utopia, given its untimeliness. It remains new in being, to the last, a *project*: Barthes hands it on, in saying that this is 'the Work I would like to write, or would like somebody to write for me today' (378). In this respect, the postulated C-major work fits Eco's first criterion of the open work: 'We can say that [the open work is] quite literally "unfinished": the author seems to hand [it] on to the performer more or less like the components of a construction kit.' (*OW*, 4) The tonal or *readerly* work that is suggested to us at the end of the *Préparation* will always have to be written. The return to tonality does not, therefore, involve ultimate resolution. Earlier in the *Préparation*, Barthes quoted Cage's analysis of Schoenberg's structure. Cage points out that, in tonal music, structure is dependent on the cadence. 'Therefore', remarks Barthes, 'structure is not planning, it's tonality (a unitary system whose unity is imposed *at the end*). The [Mallarméan] Album [is] atonal, *without cadence*.' (*PR*, 252, italics in original) Barthes figured the end of *La Préparation du roman II* not as a conclusion, but instead as 'a *Suspension*, a final Suspense, whose resolution even I don't know' (*PR*, 184, italics in original). So, as in the Album or in atonal music, there is no concluding cadence. If there is, it is what in music is called an interrupted cadence — an open ending which still engages our expectation of what is to come next. To quote from a text by Barthes on Brecht, the text, in the end, is 'deprived of what in music is called the Zeigarnik effect (when the final resolution of a musical sequence retroactively gives it its meaning). Discontinuity of discourse keeps the final meaning from "taking" '.[27]

It is possible, then, to read the conclusion of Barthes's final lecture as *open*. However, I think it is the very use of music in this final paragraph that undermines such a reading. When Barthes uses music as a metaphor, he employs atonal music, because of its readily-apparent timeliness in figuring the experience of the Text. This seems slightly disingenuous: while Barthes is happy to advocate atonal music as a useful trope, he does not seem fully to believe in its urgency and necessity. That is, he uses contemporary music as a *figure* in writing, but does not, as musician or 'man of taste', have time for it. His discussions of music itself are always focused on Romantic music. Although Barthes *suggests* the metaphoric potency of this music, he never actually uses it metaphorically. This is because it is precisely its lack of use-value, its untimeliness and desuetude that form such a vital part of Barthes's intense love for it as well as underscoring his late sense of himself as isolated defender of cultural artefacts. Barthes, for whom music is the only art-form into which cultural coding is not allowed to intrude, consistently refuses any historical-materialist reading of music. The only meaning of music must be the body, as essays such as 'The Grain of the Voice' and 'Rasch' make clear. It is difficult to imagine a more contra-Adornian approach. When music is used as metaphor — and we have seen that it is thus very fruitfully employed — it is never the music that is the object of Barthes's taste. The music which he does love cannot be employed metaphorically — but is, instead, the locus of an *escape* from sociality and culture; it is the great symbol of taste, the site of the separation which Barthes declares, in his final teachings, that he must from now on *assume*. This is why the music that is invoked at the end of La Préparation du roman — simple, desirable, tonal — is invoked '*without metaphor*' (PR, 384, cf. supra).

NOTES

1 The one text on music predating 1970, the mythology 'Bourgeois Vocal Art', does not demystify music itself, but rather attacks over-expressive 'bourgeois' vocal styling, as exemplified by Gérard Souzay. This attack is motivated by Barthes's belief that such styling betrays and bowdlerizes the ineffable, self-sufficient 'sensual truth' of music. See Roland Barthes, *The Eiffel Tower, and Other Mythologies*, translated by Richard Howard (Berkeley, University of California Press, 1997), 119–22.
2 Johan Fornäs, 'Text and Music revisited', *Theory, Culture and Society* 14:3 (1997), 109–23 (118).
3 Roland Barthes, 'The Grain of the Voice' in *The Reponsibility of Forms: Critical Essays on Music, Art, and Representation*, translated by Richard Howard (Berkeley, University of California Press, 1985), 267–77 (269).

4 Roland Barthes, 'Music, Voice, Language' in *The Responsibility of Forms*, 278–85 (285), italics in original.
5 Roland Barthes, 'Rasch' in *The Responsibility of Forms*, 299–312 (312), italics in original.
6 Peter Dayan, 'La Musique et les lettres chez Barthes', *French Studies* 57:3 (2003), 335–48 (335).
7 Roland Barthes, *S/Z*, translated by Richard Miller (New York, Hill and Wang, 1974).
8 Roland Barthes, 'From Work to Text' in *The Rustle of Language*, translated by Richard Howard (Berkeley, University of California Press, 1986), 56–64. Page references follow the abbreviation *FWT* and are included in the text.
9 Space restrictions prevent a more in-depth discussion of Barthes's thinking on this subject. For a representative example, see the section on 'L'Amateur' in the 1975 interview with Jean-Jacques Brochier, 'Vingt Mots-clés pour Roland Barthes' in *Œuvres complètes*, edited by Eric Marty, 5 vols. (Paris, Seuil, 2002), IV, 851–75. Further page references follow the abbreviation *OC* and are included in the text. See also the article 'Texte (théorie du)' in *OC* IV, 443–59, especially 455.
10 Roland Barthes, *La Préparation du roman I & II*, edited by Nathalie Léger (Paris, Seuil/IMEC, 2003). Page references follow the abbreviation *PR* and are included in the text. Translations are my own.
11 '*Longtemps, je me suis couché de bonne heure...*' in *The Rustle of Language*, 277–90 (281), italics in original.
12 '*Longtemps*', 282.
13 I am aware that, in suggesting that our experience of the *Cours* is expected to be similar to the experience of Text as postulated by the atonal analogy, I am invoking a potentially careless slippage between the specificity of Barthes's writing on the Text, which so often tends toward idealization, and my more generalized conception of the status of the lectures. Nonetheless, I am convinced that the invocation of Barthes's atonal analogy gives us a helpful analytical lens through which to view the 'serial' construction of the lectures — and, by extension, the similar construction of *The Pleasure of the Text*, *Roland Barthes by Roland Barthes* and *A Lover's Discourse: Fragments*.
14 Umberto Eco, *The Open Work*, translated by Anna Cancogni (London, Hutchinson Radius, 1989). Page references follow the abbreviation *OW* and are included in the text.
15 Pierre Boulez, *Orientations: Collected Writings*, edited by Jean-Jacques Nattiez, translated by Martin Cooper (London, Faber, 1986), 145.
16 Roland Barthes, *Comment vivre ensemble: Simulations romanesques de quelques espaces quotidiens*, edited by Claude Coste (Paris, Seuil/IMEC, 2002), 37. Page references follow the abbreviation *CVE* and are included in the text. Translations are my own. Roland Barthes, *The Neutral*, edited by

Thomas Clerc and translated by Rosalind E. Krauss and Denis Hollier (New York, Columbia University Press, 2005). Page references follow the abbreviation *N* and are included in the text.

17 Roland Barthes, *A Lover's Discourse. Fragments*, translated by Richard Howard (New York, Hill and Wang, 1978).

18 Adorno, in his writings on 'the New Music', insists on the important diagnostic function of post-Schoenbergian music in presenting the reality of modern experience, and in revealing tonal culture as a myth or 'second nature' which must be abolished in order to avoid continuing reification of the (listener's) artistic experience. See Adorno's 'The Aging of the New Music' (127–34) and 'Difficulties' (644–79) in *Essays on Music*, edited by Richard Leppert, translated by Susan H. Gillespie (Berkeley, University of California Press, 2002).

19 Jean-Jacques Nattiez, *Music and Discourse: Toward a Semiology of Music*, translated by Carolyn Abbate (Princeton, Princeton University Press, 1990), 12.

20 Nattiez, *Music and Discourse*, 83, italics in original.

21 In the third lecture of the second *Préparation* series (15 December 1979), Barthes states that 'The Course springs from my general interest — which I've already written about in terms of music and painting — in the *Amateur*, the practices and values of the Amateur. The Amateur = he who *simulates* the Artist (and the Artist would do well, from time to time, to simulate the Amateur.' (230) Thus we see that praxis and involvement are very much at the heart of these lectures, though in a different way to that figured in *CVE* and *N*.

22 See Barthes's discussion of the structuring of the *Préparation II*, *PR*,184–5.

23 Andrew Brown has convincingly shown that Barthes's last book, *Camera Lucida*, can be structurally compared to a symphony, a sonata and a fugue — the key forms of Western tonal music. See Andrew Brown, 'Subject and Counter-Subject, Some Notes on Barthes and Schumann', *Dalhousie French Studies* 43 (Spring 1996), 35–66, especially 61–4.

24 Barthes, 'The Grain of the Voice', 277.

25 Roland Barthes, 'Loving Schumann' in *The Responsibility of Forms*, 293–98 (298), italics in original.

26 Roland Barthes, *Writing Degree Zero & Elements of Semiology*, translated by Annette Lavers and Colin Smith (London, Jonathan Cape, 1984), 73.

27 Roland Barthes, 'Brecht and Discourse: A Contribution to the Study of Discursivity' in *The Rustle of Language*, 212–21 (217).

'The *Paideia* of the Greeks': On the Methodology of Roland Barthes's *Comment vivre ensemble*[1]

MAARTEN DE POURCQ

Abstract:
When Barthes starts to conceptualize his courses at the *Collège de France*, he envisions a methodology which he actually considers to be an 'anti-method', that is to say, an 'unscientific' method which goes against the grain of traditional education. He pursues the method of his seminars at the École Pratique des Hautes Etudes, especially the seminar that ended up with the publication of *A Lover's Discourse*. In the conclusion to the seminar, Barthes turns to Nietzsche to ground this 'anti-method' and to substantiate his claim that literature is a vital dimension of his research and teaching. In the introductory session of *Comment vivre ensemble*, Barthes labels this 'anti-method' — once more with the help of Nietzsche — '*paideia*'. This article aims to scrutinize the scope, the potentialities and the risks of this Greek word to Barthes's theory and ideas on life, criticism and literature.

Keywords: Barthes, Hellenism, methodology, Nietzsche, *paideia*, reception of antiquity

Throughout his work, Barthes has the habit of referring to antiquity and using notions which he explicitly terms 'ancient'. This hardly comes as a surprise, since Barthes studied classical philology and has always admired authors who had their hearts in ancient Greece, such as André Gide and Nietzsche. Barthes, however, rarely questions these intertexts or the interplay between antiquity and his own writing. In his recently published courses at the Collège de France, this is no different, except for some passages in *Comment vivre ensemble*. Barthes opens the course with his personal ideal form of 'living together' which he labels with a Greek word 'idiorrythmy'. It refers to a principle that underlies an oriental sort of monachism in which everyone lives at his own rhythm (*CVE*, 36–40).[2] Barthes's main point of reference is a community on Mount Athos in Greece, which he never actually visited: it is a fantasy of a living together located in a Greek setting (37). At the end of the second introductory lecture, Barthes explicitly points out — albeit very briefly — the presence of a 'réseau grec' (49) in his course, a network of Greek terms used as a terminological grid for the development of a wide range of thoughts upon how to live together. It is my intention to develop a reading of one of these Greek terms, *paideia*, in keeping with the Nietzschean intertext of the term and with the Greek vein of his opening fantasy. For *paideia*, which in a way is a 'pre-eminently' Greek word, allowed Barthes to formulate the methodology of his teaching at the Collège de France. It is opposed to 'method', a more rigorous and scientific term. Method denotes a single track to reach a premeditated goal through a limited number of phases, without any detours or digressions. *Paideia* entails the idea of a journey without a fixed schedule. Barthes would like to submit himself and his audience, as subjects, to a *dressage*, literally: 'a cultivation', a coming and going of the mostly unexpected forces of culture, as 'culture' is said to be synonymous with *paideia* and more particularly with 'the *paideia* of the Greeks' (34). Yet both terms, 'paideia' as well as 'the Greeks', remain under-defined in the introduction, although they are far from unproblematic (especially in combination with each other), both from a historical-genealogical point of view and within the framework of Barthes's earlier work on cultural criticism, in *Mythologies*, for instance, which emphasized the problem of *physis* ('nature') as a cultural and ideological construct that should be questioned and exposed.

1. 'The Greeks' and the Rhetorical Putsch of the Anti-historical

In *Comment vivre ensemble*, the notion of 'the Greeks' appears to refer to one large and organically developed epoch. This is not an unusual position in the case of *paideia*, as Henri-Irénée Marrou's study, *A History of Education in Antiquity*, which has remained a standard reference work since 1948, demonstrates. The book ranges from 1000 BC until AD 500 in Greece, the Hellenistic world and the Roman Empire. About this period, Marrou claims: 'For the ancient Mediterranean world knew only one classical education, only one coherent and clearly defined educational system.'[3] Differences or discontinuities are glossed over by the implicit assumption that we are dealing with one civilization: 'A civilization must achieve its true form before it can create the education in which it is reflected.' (xiii) This *paideia* is essentially a Greek one, for Marrou sees in the Hellenistic period the ultimate form of ancient education following the traditional apex of antiquity, the fifth and part of the fourth century in Athens.[4] This is the period usually implicit in Barthes' use of the term 'the Greeks'.

More than once, Barthes has denounced this kind of metonymical use of a general notion as a characteristic *bourgeois* if not *totalitarian* strategy. In the essay 'Brecht and Discourse' (1975), he explains this strategy with the rhetorical term *synecdoche*. Barthes believes that the ancient invention of rhetorical figures was a very appropriate way to map the basic practices of the human mind, as their logic is structured by discourse. Synecdoche is a metonymical figure in which one element is replaced by another on the basis of size, for instance the *pars pro toto*. This trope does not solely imply that one covering unit can absorb the other one. According to Barthes, synecdoche plays out one entity *against* the other. In order to elucidate this, Barthes refers to a text by Brecht in which he adapted a speech by Rudolf Hess, a prominent Nazi figure who is noted for the statement: 'The party is Hitler and Hitler is Germany'. One can hardly imagine synecdoches in a more telling totalitarian fashion. Barthes writes:

In his speech, Hess constantly speaks of Germany. But Germany, here, is only the German 'possessors'. The Whole is given, abusively, for the part. Synecdoche is totalitarian: it is an act of force. 'The whole for the part' — this definition of metonymy means: one part against another part, the German possessors against the rest of Germany. The predicat ('German') becomes the subject ('the Germans'): there occurs a kind of lo[gi]cal Putsch: metonymy becomes a class weapon.[5]

The metonymical formula installs a concept which surreptitiously gives priority to particular entities, making other entities disappear. It goes without saying that every act of speech entails negation and abstraction, but in this case it is an ideological strategy and not merely the impossibility of representing the real in language. When one speaks of 'the Greeks', the conceptualization appears to be less violent, because its referents are far behind us and seem to have no consequences for modern society. Nevertheless, history has proven that the notion of Greek *paideia* has remained a dominant force in discourses of power. One example, building on the previous reference to the Third Reich, may suffice: in the writings of Nazi ideologists, Ancient Greece functioned as a sort of *Heimat*.[6] They constructed an idealized model of education in Sparta, the so-called *agogè*, aimed at shaping its citizens as a function of the state interest by means of a specialized *dressage*.[7] The differences between the Spartan *agogè* and the

Athenian form of education, with its emphasis on the development of the (political) *individual*, demonstrate how an expression like 'the *paideia* of the Greeks' can hardly be maintained from a historical perspective. They are only possible in a kind of discourse that attempts to execute a logic putsch and to deny the appeal of the historical imperative.[8]

Indeed, Greek antiquity has never known a people or a state that could be called 'the Greeks'. From the very beginning, it was a generic term for a number of different entities that would belong together on the basis of ethnic, social and linguistic arguments.[9] The most influential intellectual production of what has been called 'the Greeks' is usually associated with Athens.[10] According to the epitaph of Euripides, Athens was said to be 'the Hellas of Hellas'. Significantly, it was also in Athens that the idea of 'Greekness' arose in the fourth century BC as a *cultural* ideal unrelated to people's descent. Isocrates, the famous orator who had a school of rhetoric in Athens, wrote in his *Panegyricus* (380 BC):

> And so far has our city distanced the rest of mankind in thought and in speech that her pupils have become the teachers of the rest of the world; and she has brought it about that the name 'Hellenes' suggests no longer a race but an intelligence, and that the title 'Hellenes' is applied rather to those who share our culture [the Greek term used here is *paideusis*, which is cognate with *paideia*] than to those who share a common blood [*physis*].[11]

The idea of a cultural Greek identity launched by Isocrates did not stem from a confirmed Panhellenic desire, but was an attempt to legitimate the idea that Athens rather than Sparta should be at the head of a united Greek army. In Isocrates' days, the Greek city states — despite the glorious outcome of the Persian Wars and after the lengthy mutual conflict of the Peloponnesian War — were indirectly dependent on the Persian king. Isocrates proposed waging war against the barbarians with Athens in command. Athens had the right to claim this position, at least so Isocrates' claim goes, because true Greek culture is identified with the invention and practice of philosophy and rhetoric, that is to say, with the education of the human being as a freely speaking and thinking person. Accordingly, the Greek culture or *paideia* is an Athenian one, differing substantially from the Spartan *agogè*.

Already in antiquity, then, the term 'Greek' appears to have been used as a synecdoche. Some Athenians generalized their own *paideia* in terms of *the* Greek *paideia* and expelled other parts of Hellas. Moreover, the invention of rhetoric and philosophy is historically not ascribed to

Athens but to Sicily (Teisias and Corax) and Ionia (Thales of Milete). Finally, it is important to bear in mind that the idea of Greekness had to counter the notion of the barbaric Orient. The slave ethic of the Persian people, who were subservient to the Persian monarch, is opposed to the autarkic Greek city states and more particularly to the Athenian democracy. Both culture and *paideia* are thus introduced as polemical and antagonistic terms, but also as an ideal in times when their full force no longer appeared to be self-evident. No wonder, then, that Greek *paideia* gained even more importance both in times when the Greeks were ruled by foreign powers like the Romans, and in distant regions, such as Greco-Roman Egypt, where the elite was Greek-speaking (but not necessarily of Greek descent) and the ideal of a Greek culture fuelled their education in order for them to differentiate themselves from the less cultured locals.[12] So from a genealogical perspective, there seems to be a cultural violence inherent to the use of the expression 'the *paideia* of the Greeks'.

2. The Unhistorical Fiction of 'the Greeks'

Nietzsche had in mind this complex forcefield embodied by the term 'culture' when he claimed to be *ashamed* of his own time, of the German and Christian culture in which he was living. In opposition to this culture of slavery, he posited the paradigm of the lost 'Greek culture'. His interpretation of Greek culture is primordially determined by the fact that 'the Greeks' would be creative, self-willed and individualistic. 'The Greek' is an *active* type of man, he is the artist-philosopher whom Nietzsche champions. The main idea is that 'the Greek' makes of his life a work of art. A case in point is the importance of literature for the Athenian *paideia*. The work of Homer was a constant reference, for his literature evokes a world of values that were regarded as instructive for 'the Greek' and used in daily life in the form of *sententiae*.[13] 'Life imitates art' is not an entirely absurd statement, since the pursuit of pre-eminence, by the Homeric heroes, and the active working on one's life, are to Nietzsche both characteristics of 'the Greek'. 'Greekness' as a concept, therefore, empties its signifier 'Greek' from the historical meanings in favour of an idealized and fictional *physis*, a 'Greek genius', as Nietzsche calls it,[14] defined by creativity and individuality, by the desire for *making a difference*.

Nietzsche was quite aware of the fact that he deployed 'the Greeks' as a primordially *imaginary* term. He speaks of 'the mythical Greek people' and even *the unhistorical Greeks*, as they do not sacrifice their life for historical knowledge and responsibility, but use culture for the sake of their own life. They are not overwhelmed by their history, rooted as it would have been in several Oriental cultures, and they created out of this chaos their *culture*, that is to say, 'a new and improved *physis*', 'a harmony of life, thought, appearance and will'.[15]

3. Literature and Paideia

The figure of Homer as the educator of Greece brings us closer to Barthes's interpretation of *paideia*. Homer's work was considered to be 'the encyclopedia of the Greeks'. Knowledge of different domains like religion, ethics, politics, navigation and handicrafts were passed on by his writings. It is no coincidence that Barthes speaks of *paideia* in terms of an 'encyclopedic gesture' (*CVE*, 182). Etymologically, the term 'encyclopedia' refers to the Greek expression '*enkyklios paideia*', a *paideia* that 'goes round', a recurrent *paideia*. The term is used to signify a kind of general education before one goes to the schools of rhetoric or philosophy.[16] This kind of general, albeit propaedeutic, pedagogical value was ascribed to Homer's work. The '*enkyklic*' or cyclic aspect of this *paideia* was interpreted as the repetition of the same canon of literary works, such as Homer, for different parts of the training.[17] This idea fits in with Barthes's methodology of returning to the same novels throughout the lecture course. However, the very fact that literature was put forward as an encyclopedic source of knowledge gave rise to the reproach by ancient philosophers of *polymathia* ('multi-knowledge') without the control or mastery. Socrates, for instance, claimed that it was useless and even dangerous to have all kinds of knowledge without having the knowledge of 'the best'.[18] Yet, it is exactly this encyclopedic and non-controlling aspect which brings Barthes to literature. In his inaugural lecture at the Collège de France, he mentions *mathesis* — once more a Greek term, meaning 'learning' or 'education'[19] — as a particular *force* of literature.[20] The idea is not novel to Barthes, as we can read in a 1967 article entitled 'From Science to Literature':

> The world of the [literary] work is a total world, in which all (social, psychological, historical) knowledge takes place, so that for us literature has that grand cosmogonic unity which so delighted the ancient Greeks but which the compartmentalized state of our sciences denies us today.[21]

It is precisely as a remedy for this fragmentation of the sciences and their distancing from life that Barthes wants to posit his study of *literary semiology*. The notion of *paideia* as the so-called 'anti-method' for his courses was inspired by Nietzsche through the detour of Deleuze's *Nietzsche and Philosophy* (1962), an important study that re-introduced the figure of Nietzsche into the landscape of French philosophy after decades of Neo-Kantianism and Neo-Hegelianism. The key passage from Deleuze reads as follows:

> Culture, according to Nietzsche, is essentially training and selection. It expresses the violence of the forces which seize thought in order to make it something affirmative and active. — We will not only understand the concept of culture if we grasp all the ways in which it is opposed to method. Method always presupposes the good will of the thinker, 'a premeditated decision'. Culture, on the contrary, is a violence undergone by thought, a process of formation of thought through the action of selective forces, a training which brings the whole consciousness of the thinker into play. The Greeks did not speak of method but of *paideia*; they knew that thought does not think on the basis of a good will, but by virtue of the forces that are exercised on it in order to constrain it to think.[22]

One might wonder whether this Greek *paideia* in terms of a *dressage* would not be more in accordance with the notion of the Spartan *agogè*. Deleuze seems to borrow the notion of *paideia* mainly from Plato,[23] who rejects the Spartan model.[24] The meaning of his notion of *agogè* is the idea that youngsters would not spontaneously follow the path of virtue. Because they will pursue their pleasures in unruly fashion, they must be *forced* to learn. In the work of Deleuze and Barthes, the term will receive a different meaning precisely through the mediation of the concept of *desire*.

For Deleuze, the violent strand of *paideia* fits in with his theory of thinking. In *Nietzsche and Philosophy*, he states that the act of thinking is induced by a violence and not by a natural faculty. In the beginning, there is thought, difference and the violence of this difference that causes human beings to think. It is this 'origin' in the sense of the extraction and manifestation of culture that Barthes would like to put into play by his methodology. It is no coincidence that the design of the *Cours* runs parallel with *A Lover's Discourse* (1977), which elaborates a seminar that concluded with a reference to the Nietzschean paradigm 'method/culture'.[25] Barthes structured both the book and his seminar in several dossiers which he termed 'figures' or *schèmata*, once again a Greek word. Barthes interprets '*schèma*' in a choreographic and gymnastic[26] sense: 'the body's gesture caught in action'.[27] In the case of the *Cours*, these gestures could be the motions of a professor staging his own desire to know. They are called gestures, as they do not want to name or to fix concepts (in order to develop a scientific argument) but to put them into play as *dramatic* units.[28] At the same time, these gestures attempt to keep off the metalinguistic master position towards discourse and knowledge. Through the notion of *paideia* Barthes tries to pass on the 'mastery' to the encyclopedic material, to 'culture' and literature. Their forces are capable of transforming and educating the subject. Because Barthes does not want to bypass the instance of the subject in his semiology, he creates a tension between the desiring subject and the image of the professor from whom one expects a masterly and original discourse. He tries to avoid the patriarchal position by means of a personal fantasy at the start of the course. For only the son, he says, can have fantasies, not the father.[29] The energetic position of the subject, with his discourse coloured by its *pathos* and singular knowledge, is thus guaranteed, while the unconscious is at the same time thematized as an important force in Barthes's *paideia*.[30] The image of the fantasy, however, is structured by 'culture', in the case of *Comment vivre ensemble* by Barthes's *Greek paideia*.

Curiously, Barthes decides at the end of *Comment vivre ensemble* first to give up the term 'culture' and subsequently to express doubts about *paideia* as well: 'Culture, but the word is bad'. And: '*paideia*, or to put it in a more prudent fashion: non-method' (*CVE*, 180, translations are my own). Both terms are lacking in the other courses, although *The Neutral* has a very similar design to *Comment vivre ensemble* and the idea of the fantasy as a point of departure remains. One of the reasons why Barthes disapproves of the notion of culture seems to be his *unease* with its violent and conflictual strand. Michel Foucault, for one, would claim that only by means of transgression and thus in the inherently violent conflict between the (Nietzschean) individual and the disciplinary power could (the Greek wonder of) freedom arise. In a similar vein, Deleuze in *Nietzsche and Philosophy* pleads for a more autarkic individual who is not, in the Neo-Hegelian and Marxist tradition, determined by the struggle for recognition by others but stands in his own right, affirms his own creative life.

This entails a shift from a Marxist point of view, as in Sartre's existential Marxism, that holds on to the idea of a social revolution to wipe out social differences, to the Nietzschean individualist revolt eager to affirm individual difference against the mob, which can be detected in Barthes's work as well. It can be formulated in terms of a shift from a focus on *pouvoir* ('power') to *puissance* ('potency', 'force'). In his Marxist phase, Barthes was interested in the question of how to demystify power, while in the Nietzschean phase 'puissance' is considered as a gateway to new horizons, that is to say, to the energy of the transformation of the self. Due to his Lacanian inspiration, Barthes does not bring his own rebellious or revolutionary 'ego' to the fore, but attempts to deploy his *manque* ('lack') as a creative and affirmative act. He aims to provoke his students by means of his own fantasy of living on Mount Athos and to discuss related issues. For Barthes had previously found his ideal form of research and education in the form of the seminar, in which the knowledge and desires of the participants circulate, realizing the full meaning of *paideia* as a 'recurrent' teaching. In this model, the force of difference is embedded in a community and disconnected from the figure of the master. From a completely opposite point of view, one could say that the *ease* with which Barthes deployed the term *paideia* at the start of his *Cours* at the Collège de France was inspired by his positive experiences at the École Pratique des Hautes Etudes. However, as Barthes does not explicitly motivate his sudden doubts over the term *paideia*, one cannot help wondering why he once opted for the ancient word and even very emphatically for 'the *paideia* of the Greeks'. The word must have had a certain appeal which goes beyond Deleuze.

4. 'The Greeks' and the Aristocratic Utopia

It may be useful to consider the term within the aforementioned *réseau grec* of ancient terms that gave shape to the course. This allows us to read the Greek signifier along various lines, as Barthes suggests in one of his remarks on the Greek network or cluster: 'A Greek word globalizes and emphasizes. It marks a summary, a compendium, an ellipsis — hence it ensures a productive operation of expansion.' (*CVE*, 50) The idea that the Greek word functions as a polysemic and hybrid compound from which elements can be activated, is related to the shift from *pouvoir* to *puissance* in Barthes's work to such an extent that it casts further light on Barthes's use of the synecdoche of 'the Greeks'.

Marxist discourse focused on the political usage of synecdoche, emphasizing a tactics of exclusion and absorption, while the Nietzschean view depicts metonymy as a relation of contiguity between the word and the affects and encyclopedic forces of the reader who activates particular meanings. The idea of 'difference' is not subsumed by the conflict of one class excluding the other, as in the Sartrean tradition, where the intellectual would have to assume responsibility and to arm literature against any form of anti-revolutionary conflict. Here, 'difference' belongs to 'a pathos of distances' (see *CVE*, 174 and *N*, 77), a term derived from Nietzsche which Barthes understands as 'a passion of differences, forces, desires'. Within Barthes's discourse, the expression 'the *paideia* of the Greeks' becomes the site of the desiring individual and is thus to a certain degree *depoliticized* and *dehistoricized*. 'The Greeks' are simply acknowledged as an inspiring myth or fiction in order to fuel the desire of the subject. The trick, as it were, that enables this shift hinges upon Barthes's choice of the Nietzschean type of the Artist who embodies *puissance* and who stands in opposition to the moral type of the Priest, who represents the site of power, from which literature has withdrawn (see *PR*, 383). This confirms the shift from a socio-political discourse to an aesthetic-creative discourse based on what Barthes, in *Camera Lucida* (1980), would call a *mathesis singularis*.[31] The method of *Comment vivre ensemble*, which Barthes tried to grasp with the term *paideia*, announces this new 'singular learning'. He also calls it an 'active philology' (CVE, 149), which would make it possible to give different functions and meanings to the key terms he uses, such as *paideia*. The hybrid character of the term, then, does not execute a *logical putsch*, but selects, disturbs, distorts and forgets.[32]

From this perspective, *paideia* in the sense of the 'rearing of a child' can be compared with the image Barthes uses in his *Inaugural Lecture* to present the style of discourse he intends to adopt for his courses at the Collège de France. Like a child, he would like to be running to and fro in order to show his mother all kinds of objects he has found.[33] *Paideia*, then, becomes also the Greek word *paidia*: the game of the child, the *dis-currere*, the running to and fro of the particular body that brings up all kinds of things out of a sort of affection and attraction.

In the wake of Nietzsche's writings, *paideia* and the other Greek terms can be considered as *untimely notions* and perhaps no longer *classical* ones. Literature has been freed, Barthes claims, from the angels and dragons assigned to watch over its domain in the bourgeois era.[34] The same has happened to the study of and the acquaintance with Greek antiquity. 'The Greeks' is no longer a signifier ossified by a liberal bourgeois education and its study no longer a must for the elite. A certain glow remains, however, an opacity out of its distant mystery, the aura of what once has been a 'classical tradition'.

To conclude, I would like to return to the connexion between '*paideia*' and 'Greek culture'. The very first text in the complete works of Barthes is an article entitled *Culture et tragédie* (1942). The text is inspired by the reading of Nietzsche's *Unmodern Observations*, which was one of the main references for Deleuze when he wrote upon Nietzsche's *paideia*. In the article, Barthes presents Greek culture as a strong culture, where one knew how to reconcile wisdom and suffering. Art, and more particularly tragedy, was the pre-eminent locus by means of which such a strong culture could express itself (*OC* I, 29–32).[35] But tragedy, as Barthes wrote more than once, has been lost to us moderns. The Greeks — and certainly the desire for the Greeks — had thus become untimely and anachronistic. This counter-time is on an imaginary level connected to a particular mode of experience which turns up once in a while when Barthes speaks of literature as a medium which goes or should go against the course of time and against the dominant ideologies. For Literature offers an *idiorrythmy*, as Barthes writes in *Comment vivre ensemble*. It is the opposite of the scene that Barthes witnessed one day as he was gazing out of his window: a mother pushing an empty pushchair while dragging her child along (see *CVE*, 40). Such a *dysrhythmic* feeling, as he calls it, must have been familiar to Barthes, as he indicated more and more that his rhythm of life in Paris was not in keeping with the life he dreamed of. It is no coincidence that he took the idiorrythmy as his fantasy of Living-Together. The community on Mount Athos embodies the Greek value of *autarkeia*, but as a mode of living together it is said to be oriental and anti-Occidental.[36] For the notion of 'the Greeks' has started to become more like foreign Oriental culture, since the majority of Greek terms used in the lecture course do not refer to classical Greece but to the East-Roman, Byzantian empire after the schism with the West. The Greeks, in this sense, are used as a counter-model because of their historical liminal position: they are both classical ('paradigmatic') and anti-Occidental.[37]

In Barthes's writings on theatre in the 1950s, the idea of a counter-time was already present. It was said to flourish during the Time of Celebration, providing the suspension of the Time of Labour, like the theatre festivals in classical Athens (see *OC* I, 282). One could call this idea 'the utopia of the aristocratic (reader or writer)' in Barthes's work.[38] The term 'aristocratic' is coined to indicate his untimely, distinctive, pre-bourgeois character as well as to refer to the aristocratic Greek culture. In *Roland Barthes by Roland Barthes* (1975), the protagonist declares his love for what he calls the Greek rhythm.[39] In ancient Greece, one supposedly did not live according to the modern structure of work/freedom. This modern couple is in a certain sense a representation of the master/slave dialectic in the neo-Hegelian discourse of Alexandre Kojève which has determined the understanding of history and, more particularly, of the end of history in French theory. The rhythm 'work/free time' stands for the equilibrium that is reached in the capitalist end state in which man is both a worker and a master. Barthes wants to set up a counter-space for this master/slave paradigm and sketches the utopia of a noble, creative human being who affirms his or her affects and explores them in the time of celebration, the time of play, love and art (see *PR*, 323), which are ironically the elements Kojève would ascribe to the posthistorical condition of the human being. Barthes seems to state that history has not ended, but that the ideal of the posthistorical, or rather temporarily *extra*historical being should be found in a dimension that could escape the dialectic between master and slave.[40] This dimension is the Time of Celebration which is also the Time of Writing.[41] It is a space and a time in which the subject is free to experience joy and pain, to feel his *savoirs* (knowings) and *saveurs* (tastes) at work and working. *Paideia*, in the end, can stand for the literary refuge where the subject forms and transforms itself, since literature is the locus where the historical constraints of society (the power and servility that are implied by language in the Saussurian sense of *la langue* and discourse) are loosened.[42] And 'literary' is the semiology Barthes would like to apply in his lecture course.

NOTES

1 Thanks to Diana Knight, Miriam Leonard, Anneleen Masschelein, Judith Mossman and Luc Van der Stockt for their help and advice during the writing process of this text.
2 See Roland Barthes, *Comment vivre ensemble. Simulations romanesques de quelques espaces quotidiens*, edited by Claude Coste (Paris, Seuil/IMEC, 2002). Page references follow the abbreviation *CVE* and are included in the text. Translations are my own.
3 See Henri-Irenée Marrou, *A History of Education in Antiquity* (London, Sheed and Ward, 1956), xiii.
4 For criticism on Marrou, see *Education in Greek and Roman antiquity*, edited by Yun Lee Too (Leiden, Boston & Köln, Brill, 2001).
5 Roland Barthes, 'Brecht and Discourse: A Contribution to the Study of Discursivity' in *The Rustle of Language*, translated by Richard Howard (Oxford, Basil Blackwell, 1986), 212–22 (218).
6 See Charles Bambach, *Heidegger's Roots. Nietzsche, National Socialism, and the Greeks* (Ithaca–London, Cornell University Press, 2003), 46ff., and

The Paideia *of the Greeks* 35

Katie Fleming, 'The Use and Abuse of Antiquity. The Politics and Morality of Appropriation' in *Classics and the Uses of Reception*, edited by Charles Martindale and Richard F. Thomas (Malden, Oxford & Victoria, Blackwell, 2006), 127–37.

7 See Nigel M. Kennell, *The Gymnasium of Virtue. Education and Culture in Ancient Sparta* (Chapel Hill & London, University of North Carolina Press, 1995), 3. There is also the famous example of Werner Jaeger, who wrote three book-length studies on *paideia* and sympathized with the Nazis during World War II. See Werner Jaeger, *Paideia: the Ideal of Greek Culture.* (Oxford, Basil Blackwell, 1944–6).

8 See Miriam Leonard, 'The Uses of Reception. Derrida and the Historical Imperative' in *Classics and the Uses of Reception*, 116–26.

9 See Jonathan M. Hall, *Hellenicity. Between Ethnicity and Culture* (Chicago & London, University of Chicago Press, 2002).

10 For the function of Greek tragedy in the construction of the Athenian idea of 'Greekness' see Edith Hall, *Inventing the Barbarian: Greek Self-Definition through Tragedy* (Oxford, Clarendon, 1989), 16–17.

11 See Isocrates, *Panegyricus*, translated by George Norlin (Cambridge, Mass. & London, Harvard University Press, 1991), 50.

12 See Rafaella Cribiore, *Gymnastics of the Mind. Greek Education in Hellenistic and Roman Egypt* (Princeton & Oxford, Princeton University Press, 2001), 9.

13 See Naoko Yamagata, *Homeric Morality* (Leiden & New York, Brill, 1994).

14 See, for instance, Friedrich Nietzsche, 'Homer's Wettkampf' in *Nachgelassene Schriften 1870–1873* (Berlin & New York, Walter de Gruyter, 1973), 279.

15 See Friedrich Nietzsche, *Unzeitgemässe Betrachtungen–Unmodern Observations. II. History in the Service and Disservice of Life*, translated by Gary Brown (New Haven–London, Yale University Press, 1990), paragraph 10.

16 See Cribiore, *Gymnastics of the Mind,* 3n4.

17 See Rafaella Cribiore, 'The Grammarian's Choice: the Popularity of Euripides' *Phoenissae* in Hellenistic and Roman Education', in *Education in Greek and Roman Antiquity*, 241.

18 See Plato, *Alcibiades II*, translated by W.R.M. Lamb (London & Cambridge, Mass., William Heinemann/Harvard University Press, 1964), 146e.

19 *Mathesis* refers to the act of knowing, the getting of knowledge, but also to the desire for learning, education and instruction. *Paideia* refers to the rearing of a child, training, teaching, education and also mental culture, art, science. See Henry George Liddell, Robert Scott and Henry Stuart Jones, *A Greek–English Lexicon* (Oxford, Clarendon, 1940), *s.v.*

20 See Roland Barthes, 'Inaugural Lecture, Collège de France' in *A Barthes Reader*, edited by Susan Sontag (New York, Hill and Wang, 1982), 457–78 (462ff.).

21 Barthes, 'From Science to Literature' in *The Rustle of Language*, 3–11 (3–4).

22 See Gilles Deleuze, *Nietzsche and Philosophy*, translated by Hugh Tomlinson (New York, Columbia University Press, 2006), 108.
23 See Deleuze, *Nietzsche and Philosophy*, 108n33 and Plato, *The Republic II*, 518–19, translated by Paul Shorey (London & Cambridge, Mass., William Heinemann/Harvard University Press, 1963).
24 See Plato, *The Republic*, 548.
25 Claude Coste discusses this in his introduction to *Comment vivre ensemble*; see *CVE*, 23.
26 Significantly, Isocrates considered education to be a *gymnastics of the mind*. See Isocrates, *Antidosis*, 181, in *Isocrates*, 2 volumes, translated by George Norlin (Cambridge, Mass. & London, Harvard University Press, 1991). For the connexions between the 'enkyklios paideia', music and gymnastics, see Herman Koller, 'Enkyklios paideia', *Glotta* 34 (1955), 174–89 and Hans Joachim Mette, 'Enkyklios paideia', *Gymnasium* 67 (1960), 300–7.
27 Roland Barthes, *A Lover's Discourse. Fragments*, translated by Richard Howard (New York, Hill and Wang, 1978), 4.
28 Barthes explains the idea of 'dramatization' in *CVE*, 51: 'The dis-cursive is not of the demonstrative and persuasive order (it does not intend to demonstrate a theorem, to convince someone of a belief or a position) – but of a "dramatic" order, in the Nietzschean sense: "that" rather than "what".'
29 See Barthes, 'Inaugural Lecture, Collège de France', 477.
30 *Pathos* is a key concept in Barthes's later work. See, for instance, *CVE*, 174 and *The Neutral*, edited by Thomas Clerc and translated by Rosalind E. Krauss and Denis Hollier (New York, Columbia University Press, 2005), 77 (page references follow the abbreviation *N*), and Roland Barthes, *La Préparation du roman I & II*, edited by Nathalie Léger (Paris, Seuil/IMEC, 2003), 93 (page references follow the abbreviation *PR*).
31 Roland Barthes, *Camera Lucida: Reflections on Photography*, translated by Richard Howard (New York, Hill and Wang, 1981), 8.
32 Nietzsche understands the unhistorical as the capability to forget. In his *Inaugural Lecture*, Barthes expresses a similar desire to regard the act of forgetting as a primordial force of his position as a researcher and teacher at the *Collège de France*: 'I undertake therefore to let myself be borne on by the force of any living life, forgetfulness' (478).
33 See Barthes, 'Inaugural Lecture, Collège de France', 477.
34 See Barthes, 'Inaugural Lecture, Collège de France', 476.
35 See Barthes, 'Culture et tragédie' in *Œuvres complètes*, edited by Eric Marty, 5 vols. (Paris, Seuil, 2002). Page references follow the abbreviation *OC* and are included in the text.
36 See *CVE*, 48, 49, 70–71, 79, 172, 197.
37 Greece can be considered as a liminal space between the Occident and the Orient: it can be both positively occidental (in the sense of non-barbaric and

thus a non-slavery culture, as Isocrates used it) and positively oriental (in the sense of non-Christian and thus non-slavery). Nietzsche would love to be a pupil of the Greeks and designs a new way of 'classical philology' which would by definition be antimodern. It would act against the age, in order to have an effect on it, for the benefit of the future. See Nietzsche, *Unmodern Observations II*, paragraph 1.

38 See also Diana Knight, *Barthes and Utopia. Space, Travel, Writing* (Oxford, Clarendon Press, 1997).
39 Barthes, *Roland Barthes by Roland Barthes*, translated by Richard Howard (Berkeley, University of California Press, 1977), 157.
40 Nietzsche equates the moment of being unhistorical with the experience of happiness. See Nietzsche, *Unmodern Observations II*, paragraph 2.
41 See Barthes, 'Inaugural Lecture, Collège de France': 'Writing makes knowledge festive' (464).
42 See Barthes, 'Inaugural Lecture, Collège de France': 'In speech, then, servility and power are inescapably intermingled' (461).

How to Become What One Is: Roland Barthes's Final Fantasy

Kris Pint

Abstract:
In his inaugural lecture at the Collège de France, Barthes introduced the fantasy as an important epistemological tool for the reading strategy he would try to develop in his lecture courses. The notion of fantasy oscillates between two important, but apparently irreconcilable intertexts: Lacanian psychoanalysis and Nietzschean philosophy. True to his desire for the Neutral, Barthes refused to choose between them and instead searched for a third term which would outplay the opposition. I argue that Barthes finally found this term in a revaluation of the imaginary and a plea for a return of the repressed 'ego' in literary theory, a 'romanesque' ego, which 'writes' itself in the search for a readable oeuvre.

Keywords: Barthes, fantasy, imaginary, self-creation, Deleuze, Lacan

Last summer, I was fortunate enough to visit Urt. This quiet village in the southwest of France is the place where Roland Barthes used to spend his summer holidays, and where he also prepared the lectures he was going to give at the Collège de France the next year. We went to Barthes's vacation home, which looked still very much the same as on the photograph reproduced in *Roland Barthes by Roland Barthes* (1975).[1] Of course, there was no one home there. And then I had this very uncanny experience: standing at the gate, I suddenly heard an old phone ringing in the empty house. Nobody answered, and after a while, quite a long while actually, the ringing stopped. Who was calling? And would this person keep calling back, insisting on getting an answer, even if the person who should answer this call had left the house some time ago, never to come back?

The strange thing was that nobody else in our company seemed to have heard a phone ringing, so I started to doubt. Was it not rather unlikely that someone should call this seemingly uninhabited house with shuttered windows? Maybe it was only a waking dream, an auditory hallucination — and even if it were a real call, there would have been a perfectly rational explanation. Wrong number, no doubt.

Anyhow, it seemed of no importance. Still, this phone touched a nerve, perhaps simply because I recognized in its persistent, yet futile ringing my own fascination for the texts of Roland Barthes, in which there is always somewhere a phone calling, collector's call, of course, and then this strange, unknown, long distance voice asking, in different ways, the same personal question: Why should you write?

I could of course give an answer in bad faith. Like the grocer in Sartre's *Being and Nothingness* (1943), I can always try to convince myself that I coincide completely with the role I have to play: 'A grocer who dreams is offensive to the buyer, because such a grocer is not wholly a grocer.'[2] So just like the grocer, I can pretend to be an academic reader and make believe that I only write to serve science, or, seemingly more honest, but still in bad faith, because I have to increase my economic and symbolic capital. Publish or perish, someone should mind the shop. But it is precisely this kind of bad faith that Barthes denounces: a reader, even a professional one, is always dreaming, whether it is the collective dream called ideology or doxa, or the singular dream of his own 'body of bliss', as Barthes calls it in *The Pleasure of the Text* (1973).[3] Even his interest in the most impersonal, objective form of literary theory, structuralism, is exposed retrospectively by Barthes as 'a minor scientific delirium'.[4] This dreaming is inextricably bound up with the literary experience and can in fact become an appeal, a call which turns the reader into a writer, which forces him to rewrite the text, and with the text, his own life. And it is for this call within the text, even if it is only audible to him, even if he only dreamt it, that the reader should assume the responsibility, as Barthes himself does in his inaugural lecture at the Collège de France. Unlike Sartre's grocer, Barthes did not try to hide his dreaming. He explicitly stated that this new post gave him the enormous privilege 'to dream his research aloud' (*IL*, 459).[5] Barthes's research at the Collège de France was a critical, semiotic analysis of literary texts, but most of all, as he stressed in an interview, it was an ethical research, a research which tried to find an answer, by various means, to this most fundamental of questions: how to lead one's life? (*OC* V, 740)[6]

The answer to my initial question for Barthes would thus be a moral one: I should write in order to achieve a better life. For this purpose, Barthes introduces in his inaugural lecture an epistemological tool, the driving force behind every dream: *le fantasme*, the fantasy: 'I sincerely believe that at the origin of teaching such as this we must always locate a fantasy, which can vary from year to year (...). It is to a fantasy, spoken or unspoken, that the professor must annually return, at the moment of determining the direction of his journey.' (*IL*, 477) It is indeed by stirring up a fantasy that a text is able to fascinate its reader, it is the insistent calling which a reader hears in a text and which always echoes his own desire. But however interesting the concept of fantasy may be, Barthes himself does not give us a straightforward definition of what precisely he means by this concept, which is nonetheless essential to understand what is really at stake in Barthes's ethical research at the Collège de France.

1. Maternal Fantasies

The most obvious place to look for a more elaborate discussion of the concept of fantasy is no doubt psychoanalysis. According to Lacan, our very experience of reality is only possible through the filter of a fundamental fantasy which protects us from direct exposure to the excessive *jouissance* of our organism in its reaction to internal and external stimuli, unmediated by words or images, what Lacan in *The Ethics of Psychoanalysis* (1986) calls 'the intimate exteriority or "extimacy", that is the Thing'.[7] At a certain moment in our infantile development, our experience of this 'extimacy' gets attached — by coincidence — to a grammatical phrase which keeps this Thing at a safe distance, a distance from which our subjectivity can emerge. The almost miraculous functioning of the fantasy consists in turning what presents itself as a destructive excess on the level of the real into a lacking object which sustains the desire of the subject on the level of the symbolic. As the subject is merely the effect of the fantasy, rather than its cause, we can neither choose our fundamental fantasy nor the (by definition) unrealizable desire that unconsciously directs our life.

From a psychoanalytical perspective, Barthes's reading strategy urges us to become wary of every inexplicable hesitation, every strange fascination which we encounter in our reading of a text. For it is then that a fantasy can suddenly emerge, a fantasy which Barthes defined in the introductory remarks of his first course, *Comment vivre ensemble*, as 'a return of desires, of images, which wander, which search themselves and each other inside you, sometimes during your whole life, and often only crystallize through a word.' (*CVE*, 36–7)[8] This certainly holds true for the three fantasies that Barthes explored in the four years he taught at the Collège, of which one could retrospectively say that they haunted, often unnoticed, his whole life and his entire oeuvre.

The fantasy of the idiorrhythmic living together which is the point of departure of *Comment vivre ensemble* can already be found in the very first text Barthes wrote, a pastiche of Plato's *Crito*, and afterwards appears recurrently. The same applies to the fantasy of *The Neutral*, the desire to outplay any paradigm, which forms the driving force behind many Barthesian notions like delicacy, drift or the fragmentary. And ultimately, the fantasy of writing a novel to which Barthes dedicated his last two lecture courses crystallized his lifelong obsession with literary language, and his desire to become a writer himself, which dated back to when he was fascinated as an adolescent by the figure of André Gide, by 'the writer as fantasy' as he called him in *Roland Barthes by Roland Barthes*.[9] At a closer look, all these different fantasies seem to circle around the same fundamental desire for a kind of Empire before the Sense, echoing the lost pre-oedipal paradise, a 'maternal place' as Diana Knight terms it in her *Barthes and Utopia* (1997),[10] a place before and beyond the conflicts and arrogance of ordinary language, similar to the play area between mother and child which the English psychoanalyst D.W. Winnicott discusses in his *Playing and Reality* (1971).[11] It was such an idyllic play area that Barthes tried to evoke in his lecture courses:

> I should therefore like the speaking and the listening that will be interwoven here to resemble the comings and goings of a child playing beside his mother, leaving her, returning to bring her a pebble, a piece of string, and thereby tracing around a calm centre a whole locus of play within which the pebble, the string come to matter less than the enthusiastic giving of them. (*IL*, 477)

It is indeed to this idealized and almost mythical figure of the mother that all of Barthes's fantasies keep returning in one way or another: she seems to symbolize the dream of the Sovereign Good, the ultimate object of desire. Therefore, her death, during the preparation of *The Neutral*, seriously changed the atmosphere of Barthes's lectures; they began to bathe in the melancholic light of mourning and grief. However, the particularity of this personal suffering should not conceal the fact that mourning is inherent in the structure of *every* fantasy. Whatever the fantasy we explore, we finally discover that the object of desire it creates does not exist, but is only an imaginary illusion hiding an empty place in the symbolic, and shielding the excessive presence of our 'body of bliss', this extimate 'Thing' which haunts us. From a psychoanalytical viewpoint, an ethics based on fantasy could therefore only be an ethics of failure. Therefore, all the lecture courses disenchantingly confronted Barthes and his audience with the impossibility of realizing the fantasy: he could not create his idiorrhythmic utopia, his delicate vision of The Neutral ended in deadlock, and after two years of teaching about the 'preparation of the novel' Barthes had to admit that he was unable finally to actually write one. Although psychoanalysis summons us to assume our desire, it nonetheless urges us lucidly to abandon every fantasmatic illusion it produces while we read. But in his lecture courses, Barthes does not seem very keen on following psychoanalysis in its disdain for the imaginary fantasmatic scenarios as a mere misunderstanding of the subject's true desire: 'personally, I always cling to, I favor (as the pleasure of the trap, of the *maya*) what psychoanalysis aims to detach us from, to shake loose' (*N*, 97).[12] Already in his inaugural lecture, Barthes made clear that the 'active semiology' he practised in his courses did not aim to undermine, let alone destroy the imaginary aspect of reading. On the contrary, this imaginary is precisely what he wants to elaborate upon:

this semiology (...) is not a hermeneutics: it paints more than it digs, *via di porre* rather than *via de levare*. Its objects of predilection are texts of the Imaginary: narratives, images, portraits, expressions, idiolects, passions, structures which play simultaneously with an appearance of verisimilitude and with an uncertainty of truth. (*IL*, 475, translation slightly modified)

Contrary to the frequently used archaeological metaphors of psychoanalysis, Barthes does not try to dig up the fundamental fantasy buried under the rubble of all those different imaginary fantasies which he chooses each year as a starting point. Barthes in fact takes these fantasies at face value and exploits them at surface level, 'like an opencast mine' (*CVE*, 37). Barthes has no intention of being an archaeologist of desire: he wants to be a traveller, steering a course which is determined by the direction his fantasy points to, like a compass needle. And this desire does not lead him to a nostalgic contemplation of a lost maternal paradise, but to the active attempt to create such a paradise in the future, in the guise of what he called in his inaugural lecture, referring to Michelet (and Dante), 'a *vita nuova*' (*IL*, 478). A new life, a new style of existence that his dreaming aloud, his fantasmatic reading should call into being. And so it becomes quite clear that in order to understand Barthes's theory of reading, a psychoanalytical interpretation of the fantasy can only give us a partial understanding of what he means by this important notion. It will therefore be necessary to take a closer look at another very important intertext in Barthes's work since *The Pleasure of the Text*: Nietzschean philosophy.

2. The Return of the Imaginary

Barthes's view on Nietzsche was strongly determined by the works of Blanchot and Klossowski, but in particular by Deleuze, to the extent that, in *La Préparation du roman*, he called Nietzsche a Deleuzian author (*PR*, 78).[13] For Deleuze, following Nietzsche, the real of our body is not the inaccessible Thing that it is for psychoanalysis, but an amalgam of countless different, fluctuating intensities and affects, which express themselves in fantasies, which suddenly strike us like lightning. The fantasy, for Deleuze, is therefore not a symbolic structure, but a unique event, a physical sensation which confronts us with those active forces which traverse our body. These forces, however, are usually suppressed by the reactive force of our consciousness which strives for unity, consistency and clarity and therefore tries to repress these unknown fluctuating intensities; they are also ignored by language which lacks the subtlety to express these sensations, these 'nuances' as Barthes puts it in *The Neutral*. According to Barthes, only literature, with its constant attempt to render subtle, singular events, is able to undo the reactive generality of language: the fantasies that are activated while we read literary texts, reveal to us these unknown affects and nuances our body is capable of experiencing: 'What I am looking for, during the preparation of this course, is an introduction to living, a guide to life (ethical project): I want to live according to nuance. Now there is a teacher of nuance, literature; try to live according to the nuances that literature teaches me'. (*N*, 11) This way, the fantasies help the reader to develop a taste for what Nietzsche called 'the pathos of distance', a notion which Barthes often refers to, and which Nietzsche in his *Beyond Good and Evil* (1886) defined as

[a] longing for an ever-increasing widening of distance within the soul itself, the formation of ever higher, rarer, more remote, tenser, more comprehensive states, in short precisely the elevation of the type 'man', the continual 'self-overcoming of man', to take a moral formula in a supra-moral sense.[14]

In this case, the fantasy is no longer a mere hermeneutic tool for laying bare the structure of the subject's desire, but an active programme which makes it possible to follow this Nietzschean imperative to 'overcome' oneself, to be carried away in a process of transformation, of 'becoming', to use a famous Deleuzian notion, which eventually leads to the desired 'vita nuova'. Likewise, every fantasy that Barthes discusses in his lecture courses could be interpreted as such a Deleuzian fantasy-programme, a process of becoming idiorrhythmic, becoming neutral and finally, becoming a writer. The fantasy appears in the act of reading as a 'body that I glimpse in a car taking a bend, in the dark' (*CVE*, 51) and it invites the reader to take a bend, to drift from where one is expected, to be always on the run to the other side of everything. It is this active fantasy which Barthes describes as:

> the urge to leave the very moment a structure takes. (...) Similarly, when around us — even if we have contributed to it — a language, a doctrine, a school of thought, a set of positions begins to take, to crystallize, to solidify itself, to become a dense mass of habits, of understandings, of inclinations (in linguistic terms: a sociolect), we might experience an impulse of *Xéniteia*: to go elsewhere, to live in a state of intellectual wandering. (*CVE*, 175)

The same desire fuels the fantasy of the Neutral: a desire to flee every time a certain paradigm imposes itself and forces us to choose between two opposites and therefore to betray the nuances and intensities which go beyond such sterile oppositions. Perhaps the most telling example of this desire for the Neutral is the very concept of fantasy itself and Barthes's refusal to choose between the psychoanalytical and the Nietzschean intertext. This fundamental ambiguity was pointed out by an attentive listener, Hervé Dubourjal, in a letter to Barthes: 'You can't be unaware that the positions of Jacques Lacan are in conflict with those of Deleuze. Your discourse, despite that, explicitly refers to the two of them. How can that be understood, or rather, how do you deal with such a contradiction?' (*N*, 66) True to his desire for the Neutral, Barthes did not give a straightforward answer: instead he replied to this theoretical paradox by trying to find a third term which would outplay and thus elude the binary opposition between both conflicting views. I would like to argue that he found this term precisely in the illusions of the imaginary, denounced by both Lacan and Deleuze, but reassessed by Barthes, who explicitly pleaded for a return of the repressed 'ego' in literary theory: 'The lures of subjectivity are more valuable than the deceits of objectivity. The Imaginary of the Subject is more valuable than its censure.' (*PR*, 25)

This evolution in Barthes's thinking runs parallel with a growing preference for the outmoded charm of classical literature and for writers like Chateaubriand, Goethe, Proust, Rousseau or Tolstoi. Or as Barthes puts it in an interview from 1977:

> I recognize myself as a subject of the imaginary: I have a vital relation to past literature precisely because this literature provides me with images, with a good relation to images. For example, the narrative, the novel, forms a dimension of

the imaginary that existed in 'readerly' literature. In admitting my fondness for this literature, I claim the rights of the subject of the imaginary.[15]

In a lecture at the Collège, published as '*Longtemps je me suis couché de bonne heure...*' (1978), in which he introduced the theme of *La Préparation du roman*, Barthes declared that he was going to talk about himself, and emphasized:

'myself' is to be understood here in the full sense: not the asepticized substitute of a general reader (any substitution is an asepsis); I shall be speaking of the one for whom no one else can be substituted, for better and for worse. It is the *intimate* which seeks utterance in me, seeks to make its cry heard, confronting generality, confronting science.[16]

Such a statement may come as a surprise from someone who in his famous 'The Death of the Author' (1968) had defined the reader as 'a man without history, without biography, without psychology',[17] yet already in *The Pleasure of the Text* Barthes had suggested the possibility that 'a certain pleasure is derived from a way of imagining oneself as *individual*, of inventing a final, rarest fiction: the fictive identity'.[18] And it was indeed such a 'final fiction' which Barthes tried to invent in his *Roland Barthes by Roland Barthes* and *A Lover's Discourse* (1977): from his reading of literary texts, he collected the necessary elements to create a fictive identity, based on an imaginary of writing which he described in a interview from 1975 as 'an almost novelistic way of experiencing oneself as an intellectual character, in fiction, illusion, and by no means in truth' (*OC* IV, 893).[19] But the ego of the reader which emerges from the interaction with literary texts is not a stable mirror image: it is created by an active imaginary which is fragmented, changeable and plural. This 'romanesque' ego is therefore no longer a reactive resistance to the fantasies of the body: it becomes itself part of a fantasy-programme, a virtual object which helps the reader to stimulate the pathos of distance, this appeal to 'overcome' oneself and to explore those 'unknown states', those nuances and delicate affects that traverse the body and which are taught to us by literature. Who we are is not pre-given: in order to 'become what one is', to use a famous Nietzschean phrase, one has to become the artist of one's own life, which for Barthes in the first place means to become a writer: 'There can only be a *Vita Nova* (or so it seems to me) by the discovery a new practice of writing' (*PR*, 29), he stated at the beginning of *La Préparation du roman*. Therefore, all the practical problems of writing a novel, which Barthes amply discusses in *La Préparation*, reflect on another, more intimate level the hindrances Barthes encounters in his effort to turn his life into an 'oeuvre':

> There is a dialectic particular to literature (with, I think, potential for the future) whereby the subject can be shown like a work of art; art can put itself into the very making of an individual; man is less in opposition to the work if he makes himself into a work. (*PR*, 229)

So when Barthes asks himself how to write, this question is inextricably bound up with a personal problem: how to create a versatile project of existence which is coherent and yet fully acknowledges the fragmentary chaos of nuances and intensities which make up this existence? The impasse is not technical, but ethical: Barthes finds it impossible to lie, to create the imaginary illusion of coherence which is required to change his fragmentary novelistic style of writing and living into a real oeuvre:

> To succeed in creating a novel (...) boils down to agreeing to lie, to succeed in lying (...) — lying this secondary and perverse lie which consists in blending the true and the false — finally, then, *the resistance to the novel, the inability to produce the novel (to write it) would be a moral resistance*. (*PR*, 161, italics in original)

It is this resistance, among others, which resulted in Barthes's inability actually to write his novel — at the end of his final lecture, delivered only two days before the fatal traffic accident, Barthes announced that he was still waiting for the miracle which could bring the imaginary of classic literature back to life in a modern form of writing:

> Doubtless the New Work (...) will not be possible, cannot really take off, unless an ancient taste is transformed and a new taste appears. Then, perhaps, I might accomplish the true dialectical becoming: 'Becoming what I am', as in Nietzsche's maxim: 'Become who you are', and Kafka's maxim: 'Destroy yourself... so as to transform yourself into who you are.' (*PR*, 384)

Perhaps we should recall here the psychoanalytical interpretation of fantasy: just like any other fantasy, Barthes's final fantasy, the desire to change, to create a *vita nuova*, to turn oneself into an oeuvre, is bound to run into its own impossibility. And yet, Barthes refused to renounce this desire: literally till the very last unfinished pages he wrote, an essay on Stendhal, he was looking for this ethical and aesthetic transformation to which he aspired. It is clear that Barthes identified with Stendhal, a writer who was not able to render his fantasmatic fascination for all the different nuances and affects of a maternal Italy into his writing until he exchanged the diary for the novel, or in other words, until he properly managed to lie:

When he was young (...) Stendhal could write: '...when I tell lies, I am like M. De Goury, I am bored'; he did not know that there existed a lie, the lie of novels, which would be — miraculously — both the detour of truth and the finally triumphant expression of his Italian passion.[20]

Unfortunately, Barthes's untimely death brought his quest for his own 'novelistic lie' to an abrupt end. Yet Barthes himself had strongly linked this ideal oeuvre to his own mortality at the beginning of *La Préparation du roman*. He argued there that the prospect of death was not opposed to the 'new life'. On the contrary, it made him realize that he had no eternity to create it: only in the light of its own death can the ego retroactively consider itself as a destiny, as a task, something which Barthes already hinted at in *Writing Degree Zero* (1953): 'The Novel is a Death; it transforms life into destiny.'[21]

We could compare this with Foucault's description of the Stoic contemplation of death in the summary of his course on *The Hermeneutics of the Subject* (1982):

[I]t offers the possibility of looking back, in advance so to speak, on one's life. By considering oneself as at the point of death, one can judge the proper value of every action one is performing. Death, said Epictetus, takes the laborer while he is working, the sailor while sailing. 'And what activity would you like to be engaged in when you are taken?'[22]

As the quote from Epictetus implicitly makes clear, the emphasis should not be on the completion of the task, the destiny which the oeuvre and the Novel reveal, but on the task itself, and the same goes for Barthes's fantasmatic reading strategy at the Collège de France. In his lecture courses Barthes rejected any goal-oriented methodology, because by posing a goal 'the subject (...) renounces what he does not know of himself, his irreducibility, his force (not to mention his unconscious)' (*CVE*, 33). Barthes's way of reading as an autoanalysis, which is, as I have argued, at the same time also an autopoesis, follows instead a taoistic principle: 'For the Tao is "simultaneously the path to travel and the end of the travel, the method and the achievement. There is no distinction between the means and the aim (...) scarcely has one started on the path, than one has traversed it entirely"' (*N*, 10–11). So for Barthes, every book we read, every text we write is another invitation to the voyage, a possibility of fantasizing, of dreaming aloud the other self we want to become: it is up to us to take the call, or not, knowing very well that the essence of this task lies in the fantasy itself, rather than in the completion, in the road taken, rather than in the destination. Moreover it reminds us that we do not have all the time in the world to undertake this journey, or as Barthes states, quoting Saint John the Evangelist: 'Walk while you have the light, before darkness overtakes you.' (PR, 26–7)

Perhaps that phone which I heard ringing in Barthes's vacation home, asking me why I should write, was nothing other than this ancient figure of the *memento mori*, a barely audible voice that murmurs: 'And what activity would you like to be engaged in when you are taken?'

NOTES

1 Roland Barthes, *Roland Barthes by Roland Barthes*, translated by Richard Howard (Berkeley, University of California Press, 1977), 26.
2 Jean-Paul Sartre, *Being and Nothingness,* translated by Hazel E. Barnes (New York, Washington Square Press, 1992), 102.
3 Roland Barthes, *The Pleasure of the Text*, translated by Richard Miller (New York, Hill and Wang, 1975), 62.
4 Barthes, *Roland Barthes by Roland Barthes*, 145.
5 Roland Barthes, 'Inaugural Lecture, Collège de France' in *A Barthes Reader*, edited by Susan Sontag (New York, Hill and Wang, 1982), 457–478. Page references follow the abbreviation *IL* and are included in the text.
6 Roland Barthes, 'Rencontre avec Roland Barthes. Entretien avec Nadine Dormoy Savage' in *Œuvres complètes*, edited by Eric Marty, 5 vols. (Paris, Seuil, 2002), V, 735–44. Page references follow the abbreviation *OC* and are included in the text.
7 Jacques Lacan, *The Ethics of Psychoanalysis 1959–1960*, translated with notes by Dennis Potter (London, Routledge, 1992), 139.
8 Roland Barthes, *Comment vivre ensemble. Simulations romanesques de quelques espaces quotidiens*, edited by Claude Coste (Paris, Seuil/IMEC, 2002). Further page references follow the abbreviation *CVE* and are included in the text. Translations are my own.
9 Barthes, *Roland Barthes by Roland Barthes*, 77.
10 Diana Knight, *Barthes and Utopia. Space, Travel, Writing* (Oxford, Clarendon Press, 1997), 244ff.
11 Donald Woods Winnicott, *Playing and Reality* (London, Tavistock Publications, 1971).
12 Roland Barthes, *The Neutral*, translated by Rosalind E. Krauss and Denis Hollier (New York, Columbia University Press, 2005). Page references follow the abbreviation *N* and are included in the text.

13 Roland Barthes, *La Préparation du roman I & II*, edited by Nathalie Léger (Paris, Seuil/IMEC, 2003). Page references follow the abbreviation *PR*. Translations are my own.
14 Friedrich Nietzsche, *Beyond Good and Evil. Prelude to a Philosophy of the Future*, translated by R.J. Hollingdale (Harmondsworth, Penguin Books, 1973), 173.
15 Roland Barthes, 'A Lover's Discourse. Interview conducted by Jacques Henric' in *The Grain of the Voice. Interviews 1962–1980*, translated by Linda Coverdale (London, Jonathan Cape, 1985), 281–89 (283). Translation slightly modified.
16 Roland Barthes, '*Longtemps je me suis couché de bonne heure...*' in *The Rustle of Language*, translated by Richard Howard (Berkeley, University of California Press, 1989), 277–90 (284), italics in original.
17 Barthes, 'The Death of the Author' in *The Rustle of Language*, 49–55 (54).
18 Barthes, *The Pleasure of the Text*, 62, italics in original.
19 Barthes, 'Entretien avec Jacques Chancel' in *OC* IV, 887–906.
20 Barthes, 'One Always Fails in Speaking of What One Loves' in *The Rustle of Language*, 296–305 (305).
21 Roland Barthes, *Writing Degree Zero & Elements of Semiology*, translated by Annette Lavers and Colin Smith (London, Jonathan Cape, 1984).
22 Michel Foucault, *The Hermeneutics of the Subject*, translated by Graham Burchell (New York, Palgrave Macmillan, 2005), 504–5.

'Except When Night Falls': Together and Alone in Barthes's *Comment vivre ensemble*

DIANA KNIGHT

Abstract:
This essay explores the relation between Living-Together (*vivre ensemble*) and Living-Alone (*vivre seul*) by analysing the overlap between two figures sketched out in *Comment vivre ensemble*: *Autarky* and *Enclosure*. Barthes's ambivalence towards enclosure and self-sufficiency — ideologically negative, existentially and neurotically positive — is traced backwards through a number of 1950s essays to his 1947 proto-mythology *Esquisse d'une société sanatoriale* (sketch of a sanatorial society). On the basis of Barthes's analysis there of the excessive socialization that serves to repress the reality of illness and death, I move forward again to his own autobiographical return to the sanatorium (as space and thematics) in *Roland Barthes by Roland Barthes*, in interviews and — via Thomas Mann's *The Magic Mountain* — in *Comment vivre ensemble*. Finally, some passages of *The Magic Mountain* are read through Barthes's figures *Enclosure* and *Cause*.

Keywords: Barthes, Gide, Thomas Mann, sanatorium, death, autarky

Comment vivre ensemble is perhaps the poor relation of the Collège de France lecture courses: less philosophical than *The Neutral*, less rich and less constructed than *La Préparation du roman*. Nevertheless it is the one that intrigues me most. 'A fantasy requires a scene (a scenario), it therefore requires a place.' (*CVE*, 37)[1] In *Comment vivre ensemble*, social relations are thought through relative to issues of space ('novelistic simulations of some spaces of daily life') and specifically of a utopian living space ('the Sovereign Good as concerns habitation' (*CVE*, 177–8)). Of the five fantasmatic spaces across which Barthes maps out his thirty traits, I am above all drawn to two and to the individual texts that support them: the sanatorium-hotel of *The Magic Mountain* and the solitary room of the *Séquestrée de Poitiers* (the sequestered woman of Poitiers). Whereas the sanatorium of *The Magic Mountain* 'has to do with a fairly well-defined Living-Together space' (*CVE*, 47–8), the *Séquestrée* emerges as the emblematic text of Living-Alone as a radical, unconditional, existential choice. In short, the two texts might be thought to embody Barthes's twin fantasies — Living-Together/Living-Alone — in their purest form. But this is not a clear-cut oppositional paradigm. Precisely because they are fantasies, both desired scenarios are resolutely positive and are not in competition with each other: 'from a fantasmatic point of view, there is nothing contradictory about wanting to live alone and wanting to live together' (*CVE*, 35). Noting, in his concluding remarks, that the *Séquestrée de Poitiers* is one of two 'support-texts' that have cropped up repeatedly (as if despite himself), Barthes describes the *Séquestrée* as 'the text of absolute marginality, of a Living-Alone of such intensity that the secret, barely discernible dimensions of Living-With are caught up in its path' (*CVE*, 183). It is the argument of this essay that the same could be said, in reverse, of Barthes's reading of *The Magic Mountain*: that he makes of it 'the text of a Living-Together of such intensity that the secret, barely discernible dimensions of Living-Alone are caught up in its path'.

The sanatorial community of *The Magic Mountain* — 'a broadly idiorrythmic society' (*CVE* oral, 9 February 1977) — is described by Barthes as a social idyll: 'A story which is idyllic from the human point of view. Its "blackness" comes from death, not from the sphere of affects. (...) As far as the community is concerned, it's a very civilized, humanist story.' (*CVE*, 122) Yet death and the affective life are inextricably bound up with each other: 'there's a very strong investment in human relationships and yet all in a context, against a background, of illness and death' (*CVE* oral, 19 January). Of the five texts that together support *Comment vivre ensemble*, it is *The Magic Mountain* that leads Barthes to talk about himself — 'I rediscovered in this book'... (*CVE* oral, 19 January) — and to think through Living-Together with reference to his own experience of the sanatorium:

A book I find very harrowing, depressing, almost intolerable: a strongly marked investment in human relationships + death. Catagorically heartrending. → I felt out of sorts for the time it took me to read it, or rather reread it (I had read it before my illness and remembered it only vaguely). (*CVE*, 48)[2]

Projection into the fantasized space of the sanatorium involves a psychic investment in the ultimate Living-Alone of death: 'I would say the cathected object, the object that fascinates, the Cause, the *telos* — and this is clearly visible in *The Magic Mountain* — is in fact death.' (*CVE* oral, 9 February) Not for nothing, then, does Barthes describe his 'support-text' as 'that which enables speech' (*CVE*, 182): the spleen, melancholy and anguish occasioned by his reading of

Thomas Mann's novel seem to be the bodily symptoms of the lifting of a repression:

> In the sanatorium (...) everyone's mind was on death but nobody talked about it. (...) Verbalization was of course taboo and there was a fascination with an object, namely death, which was, as it were, caught up in what I shall describe as a partial foreclosure. (*CVE* oral, 9 February)

This death-inducing tuberculosis is somewhat different from the 'painless, inconsistent disease' which was described just two years earlier, in *Roland Barthes by Roland Barthes* and the contemporary *Radioscopie* interview, where apparently you did not feel ill, and where illness and recovery were mere abstract designations in the gift of the doctor.[3] The surgical intervention of a second pneumothorax, performed at Leysin in 1945, is reduced to the real or invented anecdote of 'The rib chop' (*La côtelette*) (*RB*, 61), its black humour reminiscent of that of Hermine Kleefeld in *The Magic Mountain* who, in the interests of a practical joke played by her gang on all new arrivals, has perfected the art of making her pneumothorax whistle. Similarly Barthes's own 'temperature chart (1942–1945)' (*RB*, 186) is described as 'a farcical way of writing one's body within time' (*RB*, 35). Yet inspected more closely, the reproduced chart, which records Barthes's first month at Saint-Hilaire-du-Touvet — from March to April 1942 — belies the playful legend with its stark record of the daily reality of unpleasant symptoms, monitoring and treatments ('sputum tally', 'pneumothorax notation', 'intubation test', 'sputum examination').[4] Nevertheless, if Barthes is to be believed, to live in the exile of a sanatorium is to immerse yourself in literature and to experience the intensity of friendships. A few days before his Inaugural Lecture Barthes tells Bernard-Henri Lévy that he had endured easily enough his five or six years 'away from the world': 'What did I gain? A form of culture, certainly. An experience of "living-together" characterized by an intensification of friendships, the assurance of having one's friends constantly close by, of never being separated from them.'[5] Yet one month later, in the notes for the written version of *Comment vivre ensemble*, he will equate the Living-Together of the sanatorium with the statistical possibility of death: 'Function of the group (of Living-Together): a statistical representation of the likelihood of dying; your neighbour's annihilation as a random field insofar as the neighbour might turn out to be yourself.' (*CVE*, 80–1) Whereas the oxygen cylinders outside the doors of the *moribundi* in *The Magic Mountain* had been described by Barthes as banal, indirect signs of death, this ever-present risk no longer pertains to the indirect, but to the 'implicit' (*CVE*, 81). The implicit becomes explicit in Barthes's spoken gloss: 'there's always a chance that your neighbour might die and a chance that your neighbour, if I can put it like that, might be you' (*CVE* oral, 9 February).

It is in this context that the 1947 essay, *Esquisse d'une société sanatoriale* (sketch of a sanatorial society) is so interesting. In this recognizably prototypical 'mythology', the typescript of which was reproduced in the catalogue of the 2002 Beaubourg exhibition, a self-consciously frenetic Living-Together — 'As far as possible always together, (...) the covert motto of every sanatorial society'[6] — serves to mask the harsh contingency of serious illness by joyfully naturalizing it. The key to the *Esquisse* is what Barthes calls 'oversocialization', a euphoric illusion of 'super-sociability' (174) mediated by the bad faith of the sanatorial gang, be it the feudal 'hoax brigades' (*bandes à canular*) — whose practical jokes make entertainment the excuse for a general upping of human warmth — or their liberal counterpart, the endlessly reinvented cultural discussion groups — 'circles, art and discussion groups, clubs, so-called working parties' (175) — where the same illusory sociality (the same bad faith) is dressed up in disinterested, shared noble tastes. The Living-Together of the gang colludes in the construction of a 'a triumphant sanatorial society from which any awareness of living in exile has been banished' (172). In this same spirit, Barthes concludes his *Esquisse* with a rhetorical flourish worthy of the published *Mythologies*: 'That sanatoria are *large families* is not in question. But if of necessity you are sent to one, must you be party to so sprightly a familiarization with illness?' (177)

The argument of the *Esquisse* usefully contextualizes the polemic with Camus around Barthes's sarcastic critique of *The Plague*: 'Annals of an epidemic or novel of solitude?'[7] Though this short essay was published in 1955, Barthes would certainly have read *The Plague* at the time of its publication in 1947, the very year of the *Esquisse* (one year, that is, after Barthes finally put sanatorial society behind him). When Barthes accuses Camus of alienating the facts of history by turning a plague into an allegory of the Occupation, one might suspect that he resents too the alienation of the facts of illness in Camus's creation of a hybrid aesthetic form. *The Plague*, in Barthes's view, is neither one thing or the other (neither the stark solar tragedy it so easily could have been or an historically informed account of the Occupation): 'I believe in a literal art where plagues are simply plagues and where Resistance means the Resistance *in its totality*.' (*OC* I, 573)

Not only should illness — the Plague — retain its literal status, but Barthes's fiercest sarcasm is aimed at Camus's lyrical celebration of Living-Together as, apparently, the highest human good: 'By positing *Living-Together* as the very target of the Plague, Camus makes the Plague destroy (...) a state defined by its duration, an object of lyricism and an ethics of silence. (...) For Sartre, hell is other people; for Camus, other people, perhaps, constitute paradise.' (*OC* I, 542–3)

Sartre's hellish conception of Living-Together is alluded to again in *Comment vivre ensemble*, through the trivial example of being shut up for eternity with the irritating party at the next table in a restaurant: 'the infernal image of Living-Together: the *huis clos*' (*CVE*, 35). It is developed through discussion of the episode in *The Magic Mountain* where Hans Castorp's uncle, visiting his nephew in an attempt to prise him away from the sanatorium, escapes without warning, such is his fear of finding himself ill and being sucked into this enclosed, self-sufficient and self-perpetuating space: 'It's not emptiness which attracts but fullness, or rather the intuition of the vertiginous vacuity of the plenitude of the group. This is what fascinates Hans's uncle and this is what he will suddenly flee: a day replete with sick people immersed in sanatorial Living-Together.' (*CVE*, 70) The figure Autarky (*Autarcie*), which contains this amusingly personal gloss on the uncle's motive for flight, develops the ambivalent fascination of the 'group in a state of autarkic Living-Together' (*CVE*, 71): 'What is the fascination of the small group, the gang or the sanatorium? Well, I think it's precisely the state of autarky: see the Greek term *autarkeia*: self-sufficiency, contentedness, plenitude.' (*CVE* oral, 2 February) The negative dimension of this smug, inward-looking ethos is reminiscent of Barthes's sarcastic characterizations of 1950s commercial theatre as a microcosm of contemporary France: 'When it comes down to it, the most valuable thing my money buys me is a self-sufficient world. Nothing protrudes from this enclosure with its rearguard of formidable stage machinery, nothing opens out onto an elsewhere.'[8] Ideologically, Autarky and Enclosure (*Clôture*) are overlapping figures, in that this illusion of self-sufficiency is protected by an hermetic sealing off of the space of the bourgeois stage: 'this prudently enclosed space, sealed off on all sides, without a chink for the slightest shadow that might provoke escape, fear or dreams'.[9]

However, even in the 1950s, Barthes's reading of Autarky and Enclosure is ambivalent, and nowhere more so than in his mythology on that 'almost perfect novel', Jules Verne's *The Mysterious Island*.[10] On the one hand, to enclose the world and to pack it with one's presence is the ultimate act of appropriation:

> Verne had an obsession for plenitude: he never stopped putting a last touch to the world and furnishing it, (...) he constantly sought (...) to reduce it to a known and enclosed space, where man could subsequently live in comfort: the world can draw everything from itself; it needs, in order to exist, no one else but man. (65–6)

On the other hand, Barthes is drawn to this 'ceaseless action of excluding oneself' as an existential principle: 'Imagination about travel corresponds in Verne to an exploration of closure (...): to enclose oneself and to settle, such is the existential dream of childhood and of Verne.' (65) And Barthes slips into a euphoric celebration of the 'enjoyment (*jouissance*) of being enclosed' that is especially associated in Verne's writing with the image of the boat: 'an inclination for ships always means the joy of perfectly enclosing oneself' (66). The vast tracts of the world that the ships range over merely add to the 'bliss of their closure' (66), while the *Nautilus* exemplifies 'the most desirable of all caves' (66) precisely on account of its 'unbroken inwardness' (66–7). In this mythology, Barthes describes the ship as 'the emblem of closure' (66). In his wonderful essay on *Notre-Dame of Paris*, published in 1957, Quasimodo, 'veritable genie of closure' (*OC* I, 875), incarnates enclosure as an unambiguously positive theme.[11] Once more, the voluptuousness of Enclosure lends to the figure of Autarky an existential and poetic appeal: '*Notre-Dame of Paris* is from all points of view the book of enclosure, which is why it's a voluptuous book.' (I, 873) It is because Frollo and Quasimodo reign over 'a world which is finally complete' (I, 874) — a finite, hermetic place that is materially and spiritually self-sufficient — that 'the so very ancient marvel of every autarkic universe occurs there: a supernatural state of independence and warmth' (I, 873).

In Barthes's dossier *Enclosure* (*CVE*, 93–9), in *Comment vivre ensemble*, such is the subjective delight of 'absolute enclosure' that 'excessive enclosure' — erecting barriers of all sorts, walling oneself up, burying oneself below ground — is diagnosed as an empirical alibi (in *The Mysterious Island* as in *Robinson Crusoe*) for a neurotic pattern of behaviour and a symbolic structure: 'once the process of enclosure (...) has got under way, it operates just like a mirage; nothing can stop it and nothing can satisfy it because symbolically the only absolute protection is one's mother's womb' (*CVE* oral, 2 March). Mélanie Bastian, the eponymous *Séquestrée de Poitiers*, had 'a passion for covering herself up', and 'was only happy when she was entirely covered by a blanket...'.[12] In Barthes's inspired reading of Gide's text, this is the key to the neurosis in which Mélanie finds her happiness, in that sequestration alone 'does not exhaust the experience of enclosure. (...) The blanket (...) next to the naked body (...) represents total isolation, it's like a second skin and obviously there is a sort of regression to (...) maternal enclosure.' (*CVE* oral, 2 March) Mélanie expresses her contentment through terms of endearment for what Barthes describes as her 'absolute hole' — the fortified, stinking chamber, the crust of excrement and decaying foodstuffs, the appallingly filthy blanket — referring to it most famously as ' "*mon cher grand fond Malampia*" '.[13] And Barthes grants her the logothete's privilege of at once naming and inventing a concept:

> following her example we might use the word 'malampianism' for every affective impulse, however fleeting, that leads the subject to bury themselves, to cover themselves up, to obliterate the world, not by the path of asceticism, as in monastic seclusion, but by the path of *jouissance*. (*CVE* oral, 2 March)

In a bracketed paragraph at the beginning of the written version of Autarky (*CVE*, 70–1), Barthes confesses to finding it a somewhat 'slight dossier' that for the moment he is filling badly. Nevertheless, he feels that 'the box should be laid in place' (70), to be completed later, by himself or whoever. By reading the figure of Autarky in conjuction with that of Enclosure, I am attempting to make sense of Barthes's half-filled entry for Autarky, this being perhaps his key dossier for the sanatorium. To conflate the two figures, as Barthes himself did in the 1950s for *The Mysterious Island* and *Notre-Dame of Paris*, is to overturn the *huis clos* of Living-Together into a voluptuous Living-Alone. In *The Magic Mountain*, Hans Castorp's extreme pleasure in the regular and compulsory balcony rest-cures — ' "It's the best thing up here, so far as I can see. I wish I were back again in my comfortable chair." '[14] — is an example of malampianism that short-circuits the distance between *La Séquestrée de Poitiers* and *The Magic Mountain*. When Hans Castorp takes delivery of his luxurious new blankets, his cousin Joachim initiates him into the intricate art of wrapping himself up by winding the first blanket securely and symmetrically around himself, vertically and then horizontally. The process is then repeated with the second blanket. Stretched out 'limbless and cylindrical in his chair' (*MM*, 103), Hans Castorp is now entirely protected from the elements: ' "there, nothing can touch you now, not even if we were to have ten below zero" ' (*MM*, 103). It is a skill he will pass on to his uncle, instructing him step by step in the art of wrapping himself up; then, 'after he had got the consul all nicely mummified'

(*MM*, 434), unwrapping him and making him re-do it himself. The allusion to the shroud or winding-sheet could not be more explicit. Yet 'the unanalysable, the almost mysterious qualities of his reclining chair' (*MM*, 103) are as voluptuous as any of Barthes's finest examples of Enclosure: 'no more comfortable provision for relaxed limbs could be conceived than that purveyed by this excellent chair. The heart of Hans Castorp rejoiced in the blessed fact that two vacant and securely enclosed hours lay before him' (*MM*, 103, translation slightly modified).

The Living-Alone of the balcony cure, an empirical fact of the regulated regime of the sanatorium, nourishes — through its voluptuous enclosure — the *telos* of death that Barthes reads in *The Magic Mountain*. When Barthes claims that enclosure in the mother's womb is the only absolute protection, he adds: 'To emerge is to lose one's protection: the essence of life.' (*CVE*, 96) A fantasized return to 'maternal enclosure' is clearly the opposite of life. If it is a fantasized death, what sharper scenario — 'A fantasy requires a scene (a scenario), it therefore requires a place' (*CVE*, 37) — than the 'anamnesis' in *Roland Barthes by Roland Barthes*, where the child and his mother, alone in their bedroom at Marrac, bury themselves together under a sheet from the bed, supposedly to protect themselves from a bat: 'A bat got into the bedroom. Fearing it would get caught in their hair, his mother hoisted him up on her back, they shrouded themselves in a sheet and pursued the bat with fire tongs.' (*RB*, 107, translation amended)

However, I have not wished, in associating Living-Alone with a psychic investment in death, to suggest that Barthes is simply anticipating the death of his mother. For all the poignancy of rediscovering his lost mother in the 'Winter Garden Photograph',[15] it is the reality of his own future death that Barthes will read into the *camera lucida* of photography, and it is the reality of his own past illness that he has read into *The Magic Mountain*. Similarly, Hans Castorp understands his own mortality when he is allowed by Dr Behrens — in the inner sanctum of the x-ray laboratory — to look at his x-rayed hand: 'And Hans Castorp saw (...) what he had never thought it would be vouchsafed to himself to see: he looked into his own grave' (*MM*, 218); 'for the first time in his life he understood that he would die' (*MM*, 219). When Hans first took up residence in his sanatorium bedroom ('Number 34'), an American woman had died there just two days previously. Indeed, all of the bedrooms risk, sooner or later, turning into death chambers. When Joachim returns to the sanatorium to die, his old room, next door to that of his cousin Hans, is occupied by another very sick patient. But it is correctly predicted that the room will be 'vacated' and returned to Joachim in time for him to die there: the logic of the novel demands this very setting for the death scene at its core.

To requote Barthes, when he alluded to the unspoken presence of death in the sanatorium: 'there's always a chance that your neighbour might die and a chance that your neighbour, if I can put it like that, might be you' (*CVE* oral, 9 February). In *Comment vivre ensemble*, Barthes concludes his figure *Xéniteia* with an *envoi* on Compline, the last service of the day in the tightly ordered monastic timetable: 'The beginning of night-time: Compline (precedes bedtime).' (*CVE*, 176) Barthes describes Compline as a beautiful idea, and imagines the monastic community arming itself with courage, through a rite whereby the inhabitants 'join forces' (*se mettent ensemble*) in order to face the darkness of night: 'And I would say that Living-Together, which was the theme of this lecture course, (...) is simply a way, perhaps, of confronting together the sadness of evening. Being strangers to each other is (...) unavoidable, (...) it's even necessary and desirable, except when night falls—whence Compline.' (*CVE* oral, 27 April)

It would be hard to imagine a better secular equivalent of the liturgical Compline than the compulsory evening cure on the balcony of the Berghof International Sanatorium. As Joachim tells the newly arrived Hans Castorp, everyone is obliged to participate, every day, after supper: ' "that is the rule. From eight to ten." ' (*MM*, 10) Hans's rapid and profound conversion to sanatorial life is mediated by the two hours that are 'dedicated by the rules of the house to the principal cure of the day; he felt it, though himself but a guest up here — to be a most suitable arrangement' (*MM*, 103). The balcony is an extension—at once metonym and metaphor—of the 'solitary chamber' in which Hans will spend seven years of his life. The configuration of space — a chaise-longue on the balcony of a sanatorium perched high on a magic mountain—repeats the 'conjugation' of height and depth that Barthes notes in *The Mysterious Island* (the settlers establish Granite House, their poetically enclosed retreat, high up in a granite cliff) and that he so admires in *Notre-Dame of Paris*. Hugo's 'stroke of genius' (*OC* I, 873) was to place Quasimodo's 'mineral and spiritual womb' (I, 875) not in the depths of the cathedral, but high up in its tower: 'replacing the reverie of the lair and the cave, in a word the reverie of depth, with the image of the aerial terrace, of the hanging garden' (I, 874). In 1974, using the image of the hanging garden (*jardin suspendu*) for his teaching seminar, Barthes wonders about the provenance of 'this myth, this imagination', and suggests it is the very notion of suspension that 'attracts and pleases'.[16] Perhaps, then, in the hanging garden of the sanatorium balcony — from *The Magic Mountain* to Saint-Hilaire-du-Touvet, via a Collège de France lecture course — it is death that lies fantasmatically suspended between Living-Together and Living-Alone.

NOTES

1. Roland Barthes, *Comment vivre ensemble: Simulations romanesques de quelques espaces quotidiens*, edited by Claude Coste (Paris, Seuil/IMEC, 2002), 37. This is a scholarly edition of the very full handwritten text from which Barthes delivered his lectures (adding digressions, repetitions and clarifications as he proceeded). Amateur recordings of the lectures as delivered were issued in parallel by Seuil (CD-ROM, MP3 format). Page references follow the abbreviation *CVE* and are included in the text. Quotations from the recordings are marked as 'oral' and include the date of the lecture. Translations in both cases are my own.
2. For biographical details of Barthes's life at the sanatoria of Saint-Hilaire-du-Touvet and Leysin between 1942 and 1946, see Louis-Jean Calvet, *Roland Barthes: A Biography* (1990), translated by Sarah Wykes (Cambridge, Polity, 1994), 45–69, and André Lepeuple, 'Chambre 18: Témoignage', in *Sur Barthes*, special issue of *Revue des Sciences Humaines* edited by Claude Coste, no. 268 (2002), 143–50. For an important discussion of the literary and cultural life of Saint-Hilaire-du-Touvet and its role in Barthes's intellectual development, see Philippe Roger, *Roland Barthes, roman* (Paris, Grasset, 1986), 325–40.
3. See *Roland Barthes by Roland Barthes* (1975), translated by Richard Howard (New York, Hill and Wang, 1977), 35 (further references follow the abbreviation *RB* and are included in the text). See too 'Entretien avec Jacques Chancel' (*Radioscopie*, 17 February 1975), in Barthes, *Œuvres complètes*, edited by Éric Marty, 5 vols. (Paris, Seuil, 2002), IV, 887–906 (899–900). Further references follow the abbreviation *OC* and are included in the text. Translations from the *Œuvres complètes* are my own.
4. These are my own translations of handwritten annotations on the 'temperature chart' (*RB*, 35).
5. Barthes, 'Of What Use is an Intellectual?' (1977), in *The Grain of the Voice: Interviews 1962–1980*, translated by Linda Coverdale (London, Jonathan Cape, 1985), 258–80 (260). Translation slightly modified.
6. Barthes, 'Esquisse d'une société sanatoriale' (1947), in *R/B Roland Barthes*, edited by Marianne Alphant et Nathalie Léger (Paris, Seuil/Centre

Pompidou/IMEC, 2002), 171–7 (174). Further references are included in the text.
7. See 'La Peste: Annales d'une épidémie ou roman de la solitude' (1955), in OC I, 540–5, as well as Camus's printed response (OC I, 546–7) and Barthes's further reply (OC I, 573–4).
8. Barthes, 'Folies-Bergère' (1953), OC I, 234–44 (243).
9. Barthes, 'Avignon, l'hiver' (1954), OC I, 472–5 (473).
10. Barthes, 'The *Nautilus* and the Drunken Boat' (1955), in *Mythologies* (1957), selected and translated by Annette Lavers (London, Granada, 1982), 65–7 (65). Further page references are included in the text.
11. Barthes, 'La cathédrale des romans' (1957), in OC I, 873–6.
12. See Gide, *The Confined Woman of Poitiers* (1930), in *Judge Not*, edited and translated by Benjamin Ivry (Urbana and Chicago, University of Illinois Press, 2003), 129–74 (55, 41). This translation introduces the real name Blanche Monnier, which was not used by Gide.
13. Ivry translates this nonsense phrase as '"my dear great-Back-Malampia"' (147). However, although *le fond* can mean background, its first meaning, and the most appropriate connotation in this context, is the deepest, lowest or innermost part of something.
14. Thomas Mann, *The Magic Mountain* (1924), translated by H. T. Lowe-Porter (Harmondsworth, Penguin, 1980), 70. Further references follow the abbreviation *MM* and are included in the text.
15. See the recognition scene that constitutes Chapter 28 of *Camera Lucida: Reflections on Photography* (1980), translated by Richard Howard (New York, Hill and Wang, 1981), 67–71. The *Comment vivre ensemble* lecture course precedes the death of Barthes's mother in October 1977 (she had been present at his Inaugural Lecture in January 1977).
16. Barthes, 'To the Seminar', in *The Rustle of Language*, translated by Richard Howard (Oxford, Blackwell, 1986), 332–42 (341). Translation slightly modified.

Suspending Events, Loving the Margin: Solitude According to Barthes

SABINE HILLEN

(translated from French by GILA WALKER)

Abstract:
In our contemporary society one would be tempted to see solitude as the result of individualism. The most striking idea Barthes developed in *Comment vivre ensemble* was the way in which solitude could be lived as a collective experience. This collective enterprise was not the result of a selfish retreat devoted to personal preoccupations. It fulfilled itself rather as an action dedicated to the other. In front of this singular way of seeing, the question arises how Barthes conceived this culture of distance as a 'social' action. Is it correct to present this ideological pathway as a form of courtesy, implying that others do not need to be confronted with the inner life of the individual? Taking these preliminary thoughts as a keystone, my article explores the content Barthes gives to his so-called *socialisme des distances* and how texts of early mystical societies develop this notion of distance.

Keywords: Barthes, eremetism, Proust, solitude, voice, writing

Readers of *Comment vivre ensemble* are prompted to listen, to look up from time to time, wander away from the text they were just reading and dream about a community unlike any they have ever known. This dreaming may very well be elicited by Barthes, who weaves flights of imagination into the historical perspective of his investigations during his lecture courses and seminars. Whilst dreaming of a life in community, his imagination moves him to linger on eremitism and on the desire of certain eccentrics (grazers, dendrites and stationaries) to remove themselves from the world. Theirs was a desire for separation more intense than the nomad's, for they sought to live their daily lives completely removed from the public sphere. The dream of not being included in a community is, in fact, one of the first dreams that the text actually proposes to us.

In these lecture courses and seminars, Barthes does not give marginality the progressive connotations that have been ideologically associated with it in the past. No attempt is made to arouse hypocritical pity or to indulge the preoccupation with human misery of those who think that they can get rid of it by changing the world. Neither is marginality the object of a political condemnation, with the recluse denounced for living a marginal life outside the sphere of power. The author of the seminars clearly wants to take the matter further and does not content himself with picking up the commonplace idea according to which recluses can never escape their presence in the world. Whereas Susan Sontag and Hannah Arendt tended to believe that everyone must form the whole of which he or she is a part, Barthes relinquishes any such demand and arrives at a more neutral and no doubt more realistic conclusion. What's the point of insisting when a human being alone can arrive at a state of wellbeing? It is perfectly conceivable that someone might dream of living alone as a hermit. Must such people be condemned at all costs? Must they be stoned for their behaviour like adulteresses in ancient times?

What makes the seminars and lectures so captivating is, to my mind, precisely the way in which they defend eremitism as distinguished from the phenomenon of migration or exile. Readers who continue their reading of *Comment vivre ensemble* will come upon elements that explain why hermits are inclined to total retirement. Instead of delighting in the occurrence of new events, they are disturbed by them because too many events obstruct dreaming. And it is by and in dreaming that the hermit finds sustenance and harmony. The event, on the other hand, can lead to a number of dangers connected to power games at work in all forms of community. According to Barthes, a community necessarily involves exercising power, assuming responsibilities, making efforts in relation to others without expecting gratitude, but also (and this may be worse), submitting to a diffuse form of power, one that is hard to pinpoint, incomprehensible at times and, in any case, difficult to observe by a gaze 'outside' the networks in which one finds oneself caught.

The legitimacy of the hermit, as it is posited in the seminars, seems to hold to the following idea: the better the hermit knows the community and the harder he strives to be integrated into it, the stronger his desire to leave it, to turn his back on it. Barthes's starting point is not to see solitude as anterior to the community, but rather the community as responsible for the solitude of the hermit. The margins make it possible to withdraw from time to time. They enable subjects to find the fulfillment and peace they are seeking, to flee dreadful events and avoid excessive communication. Margins offer a space where worldly events cease, where masks are dropped, and where social status and distinctions are divested of importance. It is a space where subjects can escape the gaze of the other, where they can see without being seen, where their lives are accompanied by well-being and its painfulness can be forgotten. At least, Barthes's dream seems to suggest this possibility.

1. Dendrites, Grazers and Stationaries

If the hermit manages to recover his solitude, he regains equanimity. In the imaginary of this text, dendrites, grazers and stationaries are not alone out of abandonment or lack of love. They are alone because of the company of the other. In other words, Barthes confronts the reader with an oddity: some people seem to feel better without a community to help them. This imaginary thread is interwoven with a more historical train of thought, which tends to demonstrate the opposite. In his more erudite comments, Barthes observes the way in which communities of hermits, despite their thirst for solitude, organized their communal lives. This was because, at a more advanced stage, the practice of eremitism probably encountered several difficulties. Involvement in too many events may indeed be harmful, but there was also a danger in solitude. It was considered dangerous for society, to begin with. The recluse refuses to participate in the logic of productivity. Eremitism up until the fourth century restricted its output to the intellectual field. It provided no productive resources for the community. Furthermore, solitude was also considered dangerous for the individuals themselves, some of whom did not hesitate to put their own personal lives in danger. Their melancholy brought them to the brink of a pride-filled abyss, to a feeling of superiority to the members of the community whose problems they refused to deal with. For these reasons, the eccentric character of fourth-century Syrian martyrs and hermits was divested of its wildness and abruptness, and became more civilized.

Barthes understands that total solitude does not offer the most adequate reply to life in community. His interpretation becomes daring when, in spite of this historical and encyclopedic dimension, he opts in no uncertain terms to join the hermit against society. Society, he says, cannot bear living alongside people who choose total solitude. It will not tolerate those who deliberately decide not to participate in politics. What society does not see is that the ideal mystical life is one of 'smooth time': 'This Smooth Time must not be broken; it must be structured, subjected to a *Rhythm*, to Strophes of Work; regular time: of Rule (...) → Whence, *a contrario*, Agitation = the *Rhythm-Less*.' (*PR*, 286, italics in original)[1]

The community which expects productive or at least participative conduct from its members cannot offer this smooth time. From this standpoint, revolts against political regimes in power are ultimately less dangerous then eremitism. After a moment of chaotic transition, rebellion can always be channeled. Intense struggles eventually give way to an alternative to the disputed power or at least a compromise between legislators and those who submit to them. Early hermits, on the other hand — dendrites, grazers and stationaries — had no desire to propose a political project, save that of retreat.

How, then, is it possible to 'live together', which in Barthes's imaginary is equivalent to 'living according to the same rhythm'? There are several obstacles to overcome. The first is that of a free trade community that imposes a rhythm on the subject as consumer, producer and participant. The power of social institutions and networks operates in this case on the basis of constraint. Firstly, constraints regulate individual delays and accelerations. They also break up 'smooth time' into fragments, dictate the sequence of actions, and influence the choice of places where activities occur. They determine as well the way that members of the group can detach themselves from pre-established temporal patterns. Finally, they serve to structure 'the economy of leisure time', to reward success and punish fraud or failure.

The only answer that hermits can give to this demand for production is idiorrhythmic in nature. In order to survive, they must strive to vary somewhat the rhythm that the institution offers them, instead of radically transforming the imposed pattern. Even though idiorrhythmy is not an exclusively musical concept, Barthes presents it as a swing receptive to individual delays and accelerations. Once the rhythm is found, personal additions and gaps have a place in the whole (see *CVE*, 69).[2] Herein arises what I see as the first idea that the reader of these seminars could qualify as political. What emerges from the rhythmic dreams is a 'socialism of distances'. This literally designates a sociable behavior. Only that which tolerates and even provokes distance vis-à-vis the other can be deemed sociable. Only that which tolerates a distance in relation to agitation can be defined as sociable.

Idiorrhythmy walks the narrow path between the absolute seclusion of the hermit and forced integration in professional or family life. It is a flowing dynamic that allows for improvisation and opposes agendas and schemes. Barthes knows that his dream verges on the utopic. He also knows that neither the churches nor the fourth-century mystical communities or sects managed to establish a rhythm of this type. But he believes that this dream must be translated into some form of practical and verbal reality. Idiorrhythmic improvisation spurs art and literature to attain better results. Writing and rhetoric are improved when authors and speakers abandon their solitude. Idiorrhythmy should therefore be capable of achieving a form of visibility in everyday life, a language that involves both author and reader, speaker and listener.

2. The Voice of Proust

The fragment on 'the imaginary of solitude' in *Roland Barthes by Roland Barthes* makes no mention of rhythm.[3] It is, nonetheless, revealing in more than one respects. In 1975, several years before preparing his seminars, Barthes speaks here of his desire to write 'in the open' (*à découvert*) (102, translation modified). He claims to be increasingly detached from Marxist, existentialist, or structuralist theories in his work. Theories must be discarded because it is in the writer's interest not to wear the mask of dogma. He must write without crutches, with nothing but the help of melodies of language gleaned from texts, either read or heard, sustained by 'patches of by-passed languages (for in order to speak one must seek support from other texts)' (102). This intertextuality, more melodious than conceptual, involves risks because it no longer proceeds by logical progression.

Yet 'the imaginary of solitude' in *Roland Barthes by Roland Barthes* seems to have only half-satisfied its author. With his famous epigraph 'It must all be considered as if spoken by a character in a novel' (1), Barthes tried to turn personal experience into fiction. It was mainly the destruction of his image that was to bring him to the novelistic form. The book struggled against the autobiographical, notably by refusing chronology and linearity. It was an exercise in self-alienation, a concern that decidedly became a search for the other from 1976 on. It was as if, in this experiment that borders on the novel, he had come up against the lack of the other. As if he were saying 'I am trying to write to discover a character. But every time I try to do so, I come up against myself. To forget who I am and find a rhythm that involves the other's voice is something I cannot do.' The need for an alter ego outside the self was becoming more and more pressing. The identification with someone or something resistant to the subject who is writing can be felt as early as 1976.

The ensuing years were crucial insofar as they yielded a series of identifications pursued in view of joining the other: with Proust the author and Charlus the character. This identification with Proust's world, although not altogether new, is crucial because it discloses another dimension in the voice of the other, which it externalizes in written or spoken form, a dimension bound up with the issue of pain. How, Barthes wonders, can Proust make use of pain? How does he give concrete expression to pain in his writing? And how does a character like Charlus make rhetorical use of pain to get through to Marcel's heart?

In Search of Lost Time was unquestionably the paradigmatic 'good novel' throughout these years. Barthes explicitly declared that, in his identification with Proust, he did not mean to compare himself to one of the greatest writers of the twentieth century, but rather to use this literature as a means to examine writing. How can the other, as other, represent pain in such a way that I as reader can lose myself in it? A few elements of response are found in '*Longtemps je me suis couché de bonne heure . . .* ', where Barthes develops a train of thought that he had earlier pursued in his seminars with the notion of idiorrhythmy.[4]

The good novelist, which means for Barthes one who adopts a writing style that has a good rhythm, represses pain. Such an author manages to refrain from commenting on pain. This directive is not simply a defense of neutrality against arguments that venture in the other direction and defend pathos, for example. Barthes indicates by his idea of repression that novelists have an interest in leaving aside comments and explanations concerning pain in order to better forget who they are. Novelists have to work at not putting themselves out in the open. Whereas in *Roland Barthes by Roland Barthes* there was still an attempt to escape the image of self by way of fragment, contradiction, or deconstruction, by the end of the seventies this project of 'putting in the open' was undergoing a transformation. The need for repression was replacing the desire for exposure. Pain, if it is sincere and has a relationship with lived experience, must be rendered without comment. This reluctance or distance in relation to readers can only work in favour of a dialogue with them. When Marcel's grandmother reaches the end of her life, the narrator describes her death through details: her head rolling to and fro under the action of Françoise's comb or the body being knocked about as the uncomfortable carriage crosses the Champs-Élysées. The cry and 'emotional landslide' that this passage prepares form a moment of truth that conveys the affect.[5]

Conscious, measured repression is more effective than words in showing and in reaching the other. However, when there is no relationship with lived experience, the idiorrhythmic writer must also manage to fake the other's pain. Lying and its many-coloured carnival-like tones help shape the novel, in this case. Jean-Pierre Richard puts this concession to the novel in the following terms:

> The many-coloured [*le bariolé*] pertains to a heterogeneous and heterological composite of Truth and Falsehood and by this very fact it cannot escape a certain moral judgement. When one embarks on a novelistic project informed by this paradigm, is one not accepting to lie right from the start, and especially to lie to oneself (which is, incidentally, not an easy thing to do)?[6]

In order to integrate the other rather than find the self in one's writing, the author must refrain from producing an autobiography. Being a biographer would be better. And this is what Barthes does in asking himself about Proust's life. He wonders whether Proust's retreat after his mother's death was as natural as the Castex-Surer biography would have us think. The myth presents the retreat of the writer Proust as natural, in other words, as a rather sudden decision made in view of the immense work awaiting him. Literary history likes picturing Proust in a series of still pictures; one of these is an image of his happy prison with his bed, behind cork-lined walls, covered in loose, lace-thin sheets of paper. Proust the artist, according to the Castex-Surer manual, had reached a point in his life when he abruptly foresaw the journey before him. He was to spend the time he had left awake in his imagination.

The question that underlies Barthes's reexamination of Proust's biography is how the author's grief over his mother's death stimulated rather than blocked him in writing *In Search of Lost Time*. The death of Proust's mother seems, at any rate after an interval of four years (Proust began writing in 1909), to have been the starting point of a *Vita Nuova*. And in some crossed-out passages of *La Préparation du roman*, Barthes adds that his own mourning was fundamental to his writing: 'The state of mourning, which I mentioned at the beginning of this course, two years ago, deeply changed my desire for the world.' (PR, 377–8) The '*Longtemps je me suis couché de bonne heure...*' lecture, written just about the same time, pursues this question. In it, Barthes delves into his dream. Proust's bereavement could not have been the natural event that Castex and Surer pretend it was. Perhaps his farewell to or retreat from the world was more painful than liberating. Perhaps his biographers got lost in conjecture about his life when they wrote of his happy prison and his supposed solitude. The euphoria that the author is purported to have felt in preparing *In Search of Lost Time* masks an aberration.

So Barthes starts reading other biographies of Proust, notably Painter's, where he discovers that after his mother died, Proust went for a six-week rest cure in Dr Sollier's clinic in Billancourt, where he was treated for bouts of asthma. After his gradual recovery, he did indeed retreat from the world and switched from a day to a night schedule of work, but in a way that was not quite as clear-cut as the myth would have it. And what's more, this retreat was mainly due to his health.[7] In reality, the death of Proust's mother threw him into a phase of mutation. Her death was not simply a factual given; it was a certainty that he felt in the deterioration of his own forces.

The project informing *Roland Barthes by Roland Barthes*, namely writing at the intersection of autobiography and novel, is set aside to follow the biographer's path that necessitates becoming the 'other', adopting the other's voice. That reconstructing a life alien to the self must not fall into the trap of mythology is something that readers of Barthes know since 1957, when *Mythologies* was first published. That the good novel must avoid a chronological, linear development was an idea that he had posited from the start. What was new in the seminars is the idea that the life of the other is sustained by a rhythm of unforeseen events and contradictions that the other imposes upon me. As a writing subject, I cannot control this rhythm unless I shift and adapt it to my pace of writing.

Hence, the good novel is not the product of an intellectual decision. The genre refuses to exert pressure on the reader and in this sense it remains alien to scientific, political or theoretical ideas. To write a novel means to exercise one's imagination and Proust can trigger the reader's affect because he goes beyond intellectual engagement in writing. In other words, the pain in *In Search of Lost Time* does appear merely as an object of examination. The narrator positions himself as a subject at the intersection of two tendencies: seizing pain as a driving force behind his writing and holding it at bay so as not to yield to lamenting. The good novel is one in which the author recalls pain in order to be released from its grasp by a form of sublimation. What Proust shows, serves to gain distance from personal experience, to eliminate the overflow of affect: 'I expect from the novel a kind of transcendence of egotism, insofar as to say whom one loves [*dire ceux qu'on aime*] is to testify that they have not lived (and frequently suffered) "for nothing".⁸

3. The Voice of Charlus

Speaking is more grounded in the world than writing. It intervenes directly in an entourage, in the presence of an audience. Rhetorics and writing exclude one other: the first is a social game, a descent into the arena, putting collective issues on the floor; the latter is a solitary dream, reflecting retrospectively on what has taken place.

Barthes would rather write. In a radio interview on France Inter in 1975, he said that he had enjoyed taking part in debates when he was young, at the beginning of his career. But excuses for not partaking in obligations of a public nature accumulate in *La Préparation du roman*. The writer who is preparing to write a novel does not want to be upset. What he wants is a quiet spot with no agitation, preferably adapted to 'proxemy' and with no lightning rods to divert the flashes of inspiration. In several passages, there is a noticeable shift from a 'socialism of distances' to selfishness: 'No doubt, one has to adopt a certain harshness, which means, among other things, taking on the image of someone distant, unavailable, and ungenerous.' (*PR*, 274) Unlike the speaker who chooses to fight, the writer would rather linger in an imaginary world without repercussions on the symbolic and political order. As in his earlier texts, Barthes continued in his writings to counter ideological stereotypes, public opinion and the ready-made thinking of the masses, but his personal political thinking had lost its force. In this sense, it is unquestionable, as Antoine Compagnon asserts, that he adopted a reactionary stance.⁹

Further on, we learn that in order to write, one has not to be critical, but rather in a state of heightened readiness, responsive to one's entourage. The clarity thereby obtained allows the would-be writer to find and evaluate his or her place in the world. Lastly, public opinion does not want to be confronted with writing. It is an illusion to imagine that the public likes the author as a person, especially contemporary authors. What public opinion does understand, on the other hand, are matters of maintenance (*Gestion*): life is worth devoting to staying alive. This maintenance or continuation of life requires all kinds of practical and social efforts: letter writing, meetings, paperwork, etc. Artists, on the other hand, regardless of their medium of expression, put their lives on the line. If they expose something, it is not necessarily their ideas. What they put out there is themselves, and in some situations, they may even seek more to destroy than to maintain themselves. They burn energy without counting and without the hope of gaining anything. Writing about the world is therefore only possible when one removes oneself from it, when one reacts at a distance from one's entourage.

Barthes is not lying to himself. In the end, he understands the view of the majority looking to maintain what is deemed worthwhile. Life can be devoted to persevering and nothing more. All other concerns are incidental luxuries. But what am I to do when I am neither a writer nor a man of the world, Barthes wonders? (*PR*, 272, 288) Does living together really has no meaning at all?

It does. 'Living together' matters inasmuch as the writer and speaker do not exist without the world. In a difficult meeting in *In Search of Lost Time*, Charlus uses harsh words to shake up the person facing him: Marcel. The violence of his aggressive speech forces the listener to own up to his own solitude. In other words, Charlus places Marcel in a situation that compels him to abandon his irresponsibility. He not only loses his friend's support but also the maternal support that had reassured him in other conversations. In discussing this discursive technique, Barthes talks of a 'rupture of anaclitism'. The speaker enhances the listener's sense of responsibility through rhetorical violence (*CVE*, 215). He triggers a crisis in which the listener can no longer find the protection he or she is looking for. In short, the good speech, unlike the good novel, must target the listener. Good rhetorics accepts the challenge of vanquishing and transforming the person who is listening. For this reason, it imposes a rhythm that jolts and demands answers to its questions. Barthes sees discourse as a form of intimidation, grounded in the idea that listeners, in the right conditions, can change their conduct.

More than once, speaking in public gave Barthes cause for anxiety. Being in the world involves being intimidated by the rhetorical rhythm of the other or, under pressure from the other, being compelled to improvise a personal speech and rhythm. The speaker has no right to silence or fatigue — situations that the writer can more easily control. And he goes through several phases of alienation: What is the other saying to me? How am I to understand the other's desire? How does the other intend to use me? The lecture courses and seminars at the Collège de France no longer assign a Marxist or structuralist place to the presence of the other. Nevertheless, I find that living in community is given a more sincere and affective place in these classes, considering the amount of time reserved to human foibles. Despite the fact that the other is seemingly an obstacle to creation, at least at first sight, he or she serves as a mediation to the novel and to speech. It is by the other's presence that idiorrhythmy creates an echo for itself in language. By this presence, the other assumes the role of muse. In the imagination of the one who creates, the importance of the other knows no bounds.

NOTES

1 Roland Barthes, *La Préparation du roman I & II*, edited by Nathalie Léger (Paris, Seuil/IMEC, 2003). Page references follow the abbreviation *PR* and are included in the text; translations are my own.
2 Roland Barthes, *Comment vivre ensemble: Simulations romanesques de quelques espaces quotidiens*, edited by Claude Coste (Paris, Seuil/IMEC, 2002). Page references follow the abbreviation *CVE* and are included in the text; translations are my own.
3 Roland Barthes, *Roland Barthes by Roland Barthes*, translated by Richard Howard (Berkeley, University of California Press, 1977), 102 (translation slightly modified).
4 Roland Barthes, '*Longtemps je me suis couché de bonne heure...*' in *The Rustle of Language*, translated by Richard Howard (Berkeley, University of California Press, 1989), 277–90.
5 Barthes, '*Longtemps*', 287.
6 Jean-Pierre Richard, *Roland Barthes, dernier paysage* (Paris, Verdier, 2006), 16, translation is my own.
7 See Roland Barthes, *The Neutral*, edited by Thomas Clerc and translated by Rosalind E. Krauss and Denis Hollier (New York, Columbia University Press, 2005), 143.
8 Barthes, '*Longtemps*', 288.
9 See Antoine Compagnon, 'Roland Barthes en saint Polycarpe' in *Les Antimodernes: de Joseph de Maistre à Roland Barthes* (Paris, Gallimard, 2005), 405–40.

Barthes without Althusser: A Different Style of Marxism

Jean-Jacques Lecercle

Abstract:
The first section of the essay assesses the similitude and differences between the Althusserian concept of ideology and Barthes's concept of 'ideosphere', as developed in the seminar on the Neutral. The second section rehearses the different stages of Barthes's complex relation to Marxism and suggests that, in spite of the explicit rejection of the doctrine, there remains a Marxist substratum to Barthes's thought. The third section compares the two theories of ideology and shows that Barthes's insistence on the centrality of language allows him to offer a more comprehensive account of ideology: what begins in a form of allusion to Marxism ends up at a certain distance. The last section wonders what contribution Barthes's theory of ideosphere can make to a Marxist philosophy of language: one unexpected aspect of the answer makes use of the concept of style.

Keywords: Barthes, Althusser, ideology, Marxism, 'ideosphere', philosophy of language

The word 'without' in my title must be taken as a precaution, perhaps even a form of Freudian negation. For at the very moment when it proclaims that there is no link between the two theorists, it establishes such a link. My aim, by promoting the *coup de force* of such parallel reading, is to account for two different styles of Marxism, one which takes pride in its orthodoxy towards the classical Marxist tradition, and one which treats it with the utmost flippancy, to the point that the claim that the texts belong to the tradition of Marxism, even if intended at its widest, is dubious. And perhaps it will appear that Barthes's flippant quasi-Marxism reaches parts of the phenomena that Althusser's celebrated theory of ideology as interpellation cannot reach.

1. Ideosphere and Ideology

There is indeed excellent justification for the word 'without' in my title. Althusser is hardly ever mentioned by Barthes. I have counted five references in the index to the complete works, all in volume four, which covers the years 1972 to 1976: this compares unfavourably with more than sixty references to Lacan and more than thirty to Derrida, not to mention Nietzsche, of course. And usually, when Althusser is mentioned, he is so in a list of theorists (Lacan, Kristeva, etc.) and exclusively in the context of his attitude towards science. Nevertheless, I shall attempt, through what Barthes calls a Brechtian 'jolt', to read the concept of ideosphere, in the seminar on the Neutral, in the light of Althusser's theory of ideology, to which Barthes never alludes.

The term 'ideology' is not unknown to Barthes, who often refers to 'ideology' or 'ideology critique'. Ideology critique is one of the theoretical languages, like psychoanalysis and structuralism, that one can bring to bear upon the analysed text. And ideology is a broadly Marxist concept, as, for instance, in Barthes's critique of the Marxist phrase, 'dominant ideology' as a pleonasm and his playful suggestion of 'arrogant ideology' as a substitute (*N*, 94 and *RB*, 47).[1] And the concept of ideology is explicitly contrasted with ideosphere in the opening paragraphs of the section devoted to the concept in the seminar on the Neutral (*N*, 86ff.).

That contrast is all the more relevant as on the same page Barthes evokes other possible words, to which the term 'ideosphere' has been preferred: 'doxosphere' (which reminds us of the ubiquity of the term 'doxa' in Barthes's work), 'logosphere' (used in the essays on Brecht and discourse and on the war of languages) (see *BD*, 213 and *WL*, 108),[2] but also 'sociolect' (which convokes sociolinguistics, a field in which Marxist linguists have thrived) or even 'pisteosphere', which reminds us of Barthes's interest in religion from cenobitism to Buddhism.

My first contention is simple. The choice of the word 'ideosphere' marks both an allusion to and a distancing from Marxism, the theoretical language in which the concept of ideology receives its most interesting determinations. And even if there is no allusion in Barthes's work (as far as I know) to the Ideological State Apparatuses essay, or perhaps precisely for that reason, I shall take 'ideosphere' as embodying a rival theory of ideology, and shall try to assess the differences and similarities between the two concepts. In so doing I am promoting 'ideosphere' from the status of one of the figures of the anti-Neutral, worth only half a session in the seminar, to be compared with such figures as arrogance, assertion or question and answer, to the exalted position of the global antonym of the Neutral, the other value of the second degree paradigm that defines the Neutral. In *Roland Barthes by*

Roland Barthes, Barthes suggests just such a twofold relationship: the Neutral, he claims in the eponymous fragment, is not the third term that relieves the contradiction between doxa and (personal) utopia: 'it is, *at another link of the infinite chain of language*, the second term of a new paradigm, of which violence (combat, victory, theater, arrogance) is the primary term'(*RB*, 132–3, italics in original).

I take 'ideosphere' to be more than a mere synonym of doxa, that is more than the second term in the first level contrast. I take it to have a constitutive relation to violence (and indeed, arrogance, which is mentioned here as one of the forms of violence, is a figure of the ideosphere), to be the very embodiment of that violence against which the Neutral strives, or which it dreams it can escape. There is, as we know, more than a little wisdom in Barthes's provocative statement that language is fascistic: perhaps a whole philosophy of language is implicit in those words. And it is the real object of my paper.

2. Barthes's Marxism

I am raising, again, the question of Barthes's Marxism, or rather of his one-time Marxism, for when he writes *Roland Barthes by Roland Barthes*, his adherence to that particular form of an acratic discourse seems to be a thing of the past: in the past, he says, he had always worked under the protection of a strong system (and he quotes Marx, Sartre, Brecht, semiology, the Text), but now, in 1975, he works 'in the open', '*à découvert*' (*RB*, 102, translation slightly modified). In this assessment, which inevitably takes the form of a chronology, I have an illustrious predecessor in the person of Jean-Claude Milner, who offers us, in his usual style, terse to the point of laconism, precisely such a periodization, from the statement that '*Barthes fut marxiste*', in 1955 Barthes was indeed a Marxist (*PPh*, 45),[3] to the sombre judgement, '*on peut affirmer qu'en 1964, la page est tournée*', by 1964 the tide, to change the metaphor, has turned (*PPh*, 56). The conversion to the Sign and its science has purged Barthes from his youthful attachment to Marxism. This, incidentally, puts me in a precarious position, since I am trying to assess a relation to Marxism in a text pronounced 13 years after the turn of that tide. Yet, I shall take heart in the fact that, two pages later, in a rather embarrassed footnote, Milner concedes that if Marx no longer guides Barthes's published work, he is 'still important for his private thought'(*PPh*, 58). This is not a strikingly perspicuous distinction, all the more so as Milner goes on to quote a view expressed to him by

François Wahl, that there is in Barthes's published work a persistent substratum of Marxism. So it would seem that Barthes's texts, in spite of the turn of the tide, kept being erected on Marxist foundations.

In fact Milner's statement is contentious. Since I am interested in the academic year 1977–78, I note that as late as 1975, Barthes was the author of a published essay (in *L'Autre Scène*) on Brecht and discourse, where Brecht's anarchistic, apocalyptic, non-apologetic form of Marxist criticism is fully endorsed, and brought to bear on what Barthes then calls the logosphere — he quotes with evident admiration Brecht's reading of a speech by Rudolf Hess, and some of the themes of the seminar on the Neutral (connected narrative and metonymy as sources for *le visqueux* (the viscosity) of Doxa) are already present in the essay, as objects of the Brechtian critique by means of *la secousse* (the jolt) (*BD*, 213).

This, of course, doesn't make Barthes still a committed Marxist in 1977, not even in fact in 1975. Indeed, in *Roland Barthes by Roland Barthes*, he talks of the 'three moralisms' (the Marxist, the Freudian and the Christian moralism) that, in the theatre, give money a bad name: this implies a certain distance from those discourses (*RB*, 46). And when, in the same book, he tabulates the 'phases' of his intellectual life, the Marx and Brecht phase of his life is associated with his early writings on the theatre and with *Mythologies*, which seems to justify Milner's statement (unless, of course, it is its source). Innumerable other phases (Saussure, Sollers/Kristeva, Derrida/Lacan) follow (145). In that book, he even stages a fictional debate with Brecht on politics, where he takes his distance from political discourse and militancy (52ff.). And militancy (by which we must understand Marxist militancy) is one of the three forms of arrogance to which, in another fragment, he regrets having been subjected (the other two are Science and doxa) (47). If we follow Barthes's own testimony, the relation to Marxism is a problematic one: Marxism is at best a bygone phase of his intellectual life, at worst an imposition from which he suffered, and perhaps still suffers in 1977.

But at least some affect appears to be involved. So my second contention will be that the allusion to and distancing from Marxism which I shall try to establish in the concept of ideosphere springs from the two opposite affects of fascination and exasperation. For you can find other fragments in *Roland Barthes by Roland Barthes* where he confesses his fascination with Marxism, for instance the fragment where he declares that he was 'intensely struck (...) and struck forever' by Marx's theory of historical repetition, the celebrated idea that tragedy returns in the shape of farce (*RB*, 88). Perhaps this is what François Wahl meant by the 'substratum' of Marxism, a term that ironically smacks of the dogmatic Marxist concept of 'infrastructure'. Or we might recall the anecdote about Picasso's statement, when he was still a member of the French CP: 'they say that the Party is one big family — well, I hate my family'. The time has come, perhaps, to develop the dialectics of allusion and distance.

3. Allusion

Barthes's explicit references to the Marxist concept of ideology are traditional: they refer to the *camera obscura* and *The German Ideology*, together with the later discussion, in which Barthes takes the negative side, about the existence or not of a socialist or proletarian ideology. Barthes seems to be easy with the phrase 'bourgeois ideology', a familiar Marxist tag. This is why a comparison with a more powerful, but also more contentious, concept of ideology is interesting.

Let me remind you, with due apology for the brevity of the exposition, of the five major characteristics of ideology in Althusser.[4] Ideology is made up of 1) representations that are 2) false but 3) necessary and which are 4) produced in determined social, historical and material circumstances, and 5) embodied in Ideological State Apparatuses. Those apparatuses generate a situation of domination through consent by interpellating individuals, all individuals, into subjects. We remember what we might call the chain of interpellation, which goes from institution to ritual, from ritual to practice and from practice to subject: the subject is an end-of-chain effect.

Barthes's ideosphere shares a number of characteristics of ideology thus defined. The ideosphere is a generator of representations that are false but also somehow necessary (you can't escape — or can you? — the ideosphere: that is why it is a sphere — it surrounds you). The ideosphere depends on determinate social, historical and material circumstances, although Barthes is vague about those, and tends to subsume them under the blanket term 'Power': doxa is an encratic form of discourse. And the workings of doxa seem to involve a form of interpellation into subjects: the subject is entrapped by the surrounding ideosphere, and she needs a Brechtian jolt to avoid being spoken by doxa rather than speaking her own language. Like Althusserian ideology doxa takes the subject unawares, it operates '*à son insu*' (*N*, 87). Or rather, since Barthes is notoriously fond of the trope of enallage and of culinary metaphors, doxa covers you like a blanket or some chocolate topping: Barthes talks not only of '*le poisseux*' (the stickiness) but also of '*le nappé*' (the gravyness) of Doxa. The following quotation, from the Brecht and Discourse essay is typical: 'his critical art is one which opens a crisis: which lacerates, which crackles the smooth surface, which fissures the crust of languages, loosens and dissolves the stickiness of the logosphere; it is an *epic* art.' (*BD*, 213, italics in original) I rather like a description of language in terms of cheese ('the crust of languages').

Lastly, the notion of the subject as interpellated, as end of chain effect, is close to Barthes, as the following quotation from *Roland Barthes by Roland Barthes* suggests: '[h]e wants to side with any writing whose principle is that *the subject is merely an effect of language*' (*RB*, 79, italics in original). But there is something obviously wrong in my latest quote. In Barthes, the subject is an effect *of language*. In Althusser, and more generally in the Marxist theory of ideology, in spite of the definition of language as 'practical consciousness' in *The German Ideology*, language is notoriously absent. The only occurrence of the notion in Althusser's ideology essay is in a footnote where he derides the errors of linguists who ignore the effects of ideology on discourse—a criticism that certainly does not apply to Barthes.[5] In spite of my own attempt, inspired by Judith Butler, to add a linguistic element to the chain of interpellation by intercalating speech-acts between the practice and the interpellated subject, the question of the link between language and ideology, which is central to Barthes, is at best marginal in the Marxist tradition.[6] It would appear that my allusion is fading into the distance.

4. Distance

Let us, therefore, go back to the moment the concept of 'ideosphere' is introduced in the Seminar: '*Ideosphere*: word I forge out of *ideology*: the linguistic system of an ideology, with this caveat from the outset that makes the definition already inexact: in my view, ideology, no matter which, is and is only language: it's a discourse, a type of discourse.' (*N*, 86) What is central in this definition is what is totally absent in Althusser, and only mentioned *en passant* and tentatively in Macherey:[7] the linguistic essence of ideology. And the gap thus opened immediately widens, for if ideosphere is discursive, and languages or discourses multiple and divided (this is the subject of the essay

'The War of Languages'), then ideosphere soon takes a plural form ('in a given world, one would unfailingly discover several coexisting ideospheres, each one intelligible to the other but not communicating' (N, 87)), whereas ideology in Althusser remains strictly in the singular.

The gap becomes an abyss as we discover that ideospheres are 'gregarious but eponymous' (and we are now moving from encratic discourse, which is characteristic of Doxa, to what Barthes used to call strong, or acratic discourses: the ideosphere covers both encratic and acratic discourses, which leaves 'the text of bliss' as the only way out). So we find ourselves burdened with a Freud ideosphere, a Marx ideosphere, perhaps even a Saussure ideosphere (although Barthes is too canny to embark the founder of scientific semiology on the ship of acratic discourse). And in each case the glorious moment of the acratic revelation of a new, and strong, language falls back into the stupidity, which is also a form of strength, of the disciples.

The gap is now wide enough for the (Althusserian) Marxist to put up a number of objections. The time has come to measure the distance that such distancing reaches. First, a Marxist would say that the concept of ideosphere privileges the pejorative aspect of ideology (ideology as error) over its necessary aspect, a failing against which Althusser was protected, at least in his ideology essay (as opposed to an earlier, more scientistic notion of ideology) by his Spinozist conception of error. Here, it would be interesting to systematically contrast the concept of doxa in Barthes with the concepts of 'common sense' and 'good sense' in Gramsci.

The Althusserian Marxist could not object to the opening of Barthes's definition of the ideosphere, 'Strong discursive system...', since in Althusserian ideology, representations are systematic. But he would object that by using the system of *langue* as a model for the system of discourse, Barthes runs the risk of fetishizing what is primarily a process, the process of interpellation—the trouble with Althusser's theory here being the one-sided and therefore deterministic aspect of the process (ideology interpellates *all* individuals into subjects), but then one can always invoke a concept of counter-interpellation, as I did following Judith Butler.[8]

The Marxist would also object that the ideosphere is not sufficiently historicized, or historicized in the wrong way, its origin being ascribed to individual talent rather than tradition (hence its eponymous character). Whereas in Althusser if, on the one hand, ideology as a category is a-historical, even 'eternal', like the unconscious (I take this as an insistence on the idea that ideology is necessary, that there is no escape from it, even in the guise of the Barthesian mythologist), on the other hand the Ideological State Apparatuses are situated in concrete social formations and determinate historical conjunctures (hence the historically variable roles of the religious and the school ideological apparatuses).

Lastly, a Marxist could object that by making the ideosphere 'gregarious but eponymous', Barthes makes it difficult for us to understand the anonymity of Doxa: stereotypes are rarely ascribable to an eponymous ideosphere, and the more embedded in language they are, the less their original eponymousness is perceived (we could mention the history of the word 'temperature' in our language). Not to mention the vast anonymous mass of the sedimentation of common sense, and the work of what I have called elsewhere 'the unknown coiner'.[9]

Barthes, of course, could easily dismiss that critique and remind the Marxist, Althusserian or otherwise, that having no theory of language he cannot understand the concrete workings of ideology, which Barthes tackled as early as *Mythologies*, as a result of which he cannot explain the concrete workings of the process of interpellation, whereas Barthes's awareness of the workings of language and interlocution, for instance in his analysis of what Bernard Comment calls 'the machinery of meaning' (language as *added*, as in connotation, as *connected*, as in narrative, as *thrust* upon the hearer or reader, as in intimidation, as *imposed*, as in the fascistic tendencies of lexicon and syntax)[10] does just that. Nor can the Marxist really avoid the determinism of an interpellation that equally affects all individuals, whereas from the Brechtian 'jolt' to the desire of the Neutral, Barthes, by trying to think a possible 'exemption' from meaning and its machinery, is trying to give concrete contents to what I have called counter-interpellation: the Neutral is the true antidote to the determinism that Althusser, because he ignores language (including in the active sense of the term), cannot entirely avoid.

The question then becomes not what benefits Barthes might derive from a persisting interest in or adherence to a form of Marxism, but what benefit can a Marxist derive from Barthes's concept of ideosphere as language.

5. Barthes and Marxism

Marxism is the site from which I speak. I am not a specialist of Barthes, even if I am a persistent reader, and as the author of a book entitled

A Marxist Philosophy of Language,[11] where I raise high the red flag of nostalgia, I am directly interested (in so far as I am trying to construct what is sadly lacking in Marxism) in the philosophy of language that can be derived from Barthes's work, in which the concept of ideosphere plays a prominent role. If the question is: 'what can Barthes teach me?', the answer has to be: 'a considerable amount'.

There are historical reasons for Althusser's conspicuous ignorance of language. The main one is the freeze on discussion of language in Marxist terms that followed Stalin's intervention in 1950,[12] all the more so as it was well received by professional linguists who were also militant communists, like Marcel Cohen, since it protected them from the leftist exaggerations of the *'science bourgeoise, science prolétarienne'* polemics, and by getting rid of the somewhat demented linguistics of Nikolai Marr, it spared linguists the equivalent of a Lysenko affair. It is not until the resuscitation of Volosinov, a renewed interest in Gramsci's philological training, and the pervading influence of Bakhtin that language found its place in Marxist discussions. At the time of Althusser's ideology essay, any attempt at treating language as an important component of the superstructure smacked of idealism (this is the rationale behind Althusser's already mentioned footnote). And it is clear that Barthes's concept of language is implicitly directed against Stalin's view that language is a neutral tool of communication rather than a part of the superstructure. Barthes's insistence, in his essay on 'The War of Languages', on the division of languages and his critique of the role of the standard, national language as organizing inter-comprehension but not intercommunication is a good instance of this (*WL*, 107) (the essay on 'Mythology Today' already contained an allusion to Marr, and to language, according to Stalin, as a 'reserve', free of ideology).[13] The time has come, therefore, to give an assessment of what Barthes can teach the Marxist philosopher of language.

First, Barthes's concept of ideosphere as language, as sticky as chewing-gum, described through the usual trope of enallage (*le visqueux, le poisseux, le nappé*), enables us to think the specific form of violence exerted by the machinery of meaning: not the physical violence by the apparatuses of repression, but the soft, symbolic violence of language, the violence of assertion, of arrogance, of the complete sentence. The violence that goes with what is said in so far as it goes without saying, as Barthes suggests in *Roland Barthes by Roland Barthes*: 'he could not get away from the grim notion that true violence is that of the *self-evident* [*ce qui va de soi*]: what is evident is violent, even if this evidence is gently, liberally, democratically represented' (*RB*, 85, italics in original).

Secondly, his concept of 'intimidation', as part of the machinery of meaning, may give more precise contents to the operation of interpellation, which to me is at the core of a Marxist philosophy of language. I shall not insist on this, as it was also, rather successfully, developed by Bourdieu in his texts on language[14] — not to mention the concept of 'place' in Flahault, whom Barthes prefaced and often mentions.[15]

Thirdly, Barthes's concept of language as divided enables us to understand the ideological or doxic nature of the concept of communication, central to all variants of linguistics as a component of what Althusser calls a spontaneous philosophy for scientists — but then Barthes himself claims to practice a 'metaphorical' form of linguistics (*RB*, 124). The concept of 'interlocutionary incommunication' used about the standard or national language in the essay on the division of languages is a good instance of this.[16]

Lastly (an end both arbitrary and provisional) the contrast between the ideosphere and the Neutral offers the Marxist a protection against her Marxism. It traces the genealogy of the stupidity engendered by a discourse which, being a strong, acratic discourse condemns the disciples we all are to a certain extent to a form of *bêtise* (stupidity). This point is made quite forcefully in the essay on the war of languages (*WL*, 108).

6. Conclusion: A Different Style of Marxism

I realize that by retroactively assessing Barthes's relation to Marxism from the vantage point of the seminar on the Neutral, I have been revisiting the intellectual history of French Marxism, in its two main strands, the scientistic/structuralist strand associated with Althusser, and the humanistic/historicist strand sadly associated with the woolly humanism of Garaudy, but which has more glorious versions in the wider tradition (as the names of Gramsci, Brecht and the early Lukacs suggest). Barthes's distancing himself from Marxism is a way out of the *aporias* of this *face à face*. By moving first into the scientific non-Marxism of semiology and going beyond this into a utopian longing for the Neutral (the concepts of *écriture* (writing) and *jouissance* (bliss) also come to mind), that is by going beyond structural linguistics into the interlocutory linguistics of enunciation, he suggests a path away from the objectivism of 'scientific' Marxism and from the subjectivism of reification and alienation. Perhaps this is where we shall find the substratum of Marxism that Milner concedes: not the positive Marxism that thinks in terms of a fetishized structure, but the negative Marxism that thinks in terms of the defetishization of language. This is where the longing for the Neutral and the transparency of language become of paramount importance. Here I should quote the page in *Roland Barthes by Roland Barthes* where he assesses his own work in terms of the opacity of social relations (a clear reference to his Marxist origins) as embodied in the stereotype, and the tender and utopian longing for the transparency of social relations through a form of interlocution freed from the machinery of meaning (*RB*, 138).

This is where the concept of style, 'the beginning of écriture', (*RB*, 76) is essential, as it is the vector of that utopian movement towards the transparency of social relations and a language exempted from meaning. What Barthes has to offer the Marxist is not so much a different style of Marxism as a Marxism that concerns itself with the question of style.

NOTES

1. Roland Barthes, *The Neutral*, edited by Thomas Clerc and translated by Rosalind E. Krauss and Denis Hollier (New York, Columbia University Press, 2005) and *Roland Barthes by Roland Barthes* (1975), translated by Richard Howard (New York, Hill and Wang, 1977). Page references follow the abbreviations *N* and *RB* respectively and are included in the text.
2. See Roland Barthes, 'Brecht and Discourse: A Contribution to the Study of Discursivity' and 'The War of Languages' in *The Rustle of Language*, translated by Richard Howard (Oxford, Basil Blackwell, 1986), 212–22 and 106–10. Page references follow the abbreviations *BD* and *WL* respectively and are included in the text.
3. J.C. Milner, *Le Pas philosophique de Roland Barthes* (Lagrasse, Verdier, 2003) Page references follow the abbreviation *PPh* and are included in the text.
4. See Louis Althusser, 'Ideology and Ideological State Apparatuses' in *Lenin and Philosophy and other Essays*, translated by Ben Brewster (London, New Left Books, 1971), 127–88.
5. Althusser, 'Ideology and Ideological State Apparatuses', 172n16.
6. Jean-Jacques Lecercle, *Interpretation as Pragmatics* (Basingstoke, Macmillan, 1999); Judith Butler, *The Psychic Life of Power* (Stanford, Stanford University Press, 1997) and *Excitable Speech* (London, Routledge, 1997).
7. See Pierre Macherey, *A Theory of Literary Production*, translated by Geoffrey Wall (London, Routledge, 2006), 68–9, where he remarks in an aside that language and ideology may not be that different.

8   See Lecercle, *Interpretation as Pragmatics*.
9   Jean-Jacques Lecercle, *The Violence of Language* (London, Routledge, 1990).
10 See Bernard Comment, *Roland Barthes, vers le neutre* (Paris, Bourgois, 1991), 44ff.
11 Jean-Jacques Lecercle, *A Marxist Philosophy of Language*, translated by Gregory Elliott (Leiden & Boston, Brill, 2006).
12 See Joseph Stalin, *Marxism and Problems of Linguistics* (Peking, Foreign Languages Press, 1972).
13 Roland Barthes, 'Myth Today' in *A Barthes Reader*, edited by Susan Sontag (New York, Hill and Wang, 1982), 93–149 (148).
14 Pierre Bourdieu, *Language and Symbolic Power*, translated by Gino Raymond and Matthew Adamson (Cambridge (Mass.), Harvard University Press, 1991).
15 François Flahault, *La Parole intermédiaire* (Paris, Seuil, 1978).
16 Roland Barthes, 'The Division of Languages' in *The Rustle of Language*, 111–26, (116).

The 'Inkredible' Roland Barthes

Neil Badmington

Abstract:
The opening of the fourth session of *The Neutral*—the course given by Roland Barthes at the Collège de France in 1977–8—is marked by a dramatic spillage of ink. Rather than take this as an incidental, trivial moment, I read it as one of the many 'ink blots' that colour the work of Barthes. Tracing his 'almost obsessive relation to writing instruments' and the material act of inscription, this essay relates the 'ink blots' to the development of a 'non-arrogant', non-expressive, non-idealistic theory of language in *The Neutral* and other texts by Barthes.

Keywords: Barthes, ink, writing, writing instruments, Saussure, arrogance

> *Writing, expression of personality? Really? I myself have three writings, according to which I write texts, take notes, or correspond.*
>
> Roland Barthes, 'Variations sur l'écriture' (*OC* IV, 280).[1]

1. 'Inkidents'

History repeats itself, but not quite as Marx imagined.

It is well known that, on 25 February 1980, just two days after delivering the final lecture of his course about the preparation of the novel at the Collège de France, Roland Barthes was involved in the accident that would bring his life to an end.[2] What has received much less attention, however, is an accident in which Barthes was caught up almost two years earlier. Quite unlike the tragedy of February 1980, the earlier incident had a decidedly farcical quality, and thus curiously inverted Marx's famous remark about the tendency of history to repeat itself, first as tragedy, and only later as farce:[3]

Thursday, March 9 [1978], fine afternoon, I go out to buy some colours (Sennelier inks) → bottles of pigment: following my taste for the names (golden yellow, sky blue, brilliant green, purple, sun yellow, cartham pink—a rather intense pink), I buy sixteen bottles. In putting them away, I knock one over: in sponging up, I make a new mess: little domestic complications.... And now, I am going to give you the official name of the spilled colour, a name printed on the small bottle (as on the others vermilion, turquoise, etc.): it was the colour called Neutral (obviously I had opened this bottle first to see what kind of colour was this Neutral about which I am going to be speaking for thirteen weeks). (N, 48)[4]

The course of 1977–8, in other words, is coloured by an incident involving ink (an 'inkident', perhaps). Although the spillage comes out of the blue, I want to suggest that it is not an isolated moment. It seems to me, rather, that Barthes's vast and diverse body of work is covered with what might be called 'ink blots', by which I mean points at which an obsession with the materials and materiality of writing leaves its mark.[5] Because an exhaustive inventory would soak up too much space, I will limit my ink quest to a few notable spillages. In 1970, a section of *Empire of Signs* celebrated the delights of a Japanese stationery shop, the 'site and catalogue of things necessary to writing'.[6] *The Neutral* would later record Barthes's unflagging 'drive to purchase' (N, 150), and this compulsion clearly figures in *Empire of Signs*, where he lovingly details how pens, brushes, inkstones, paper, and techniques of inscription change with the movement from West to East:

Everything, in the instrumentation, is directed toward the paradox of an irreversible and fragile writing, which is simultaneously, contradictorily, incision and glissade; papers of a thousand kinds, many of which hint, in their texture powdered with pale straws, with crushed stems, at their fibrous origin; notebooks whose pages are folded double, like those of a book which has not been cut so that writing moves across a luxury of surfaces and never runs, ignorant of the metonymic impregnation of the right and wrong side of the page (it is traced across a void): palimpsest, the erased stroke which thereby becomes a secret, is impossible. (86)

Three years later, however, came two much larger ink blots. In September 1973, Barthes gave an interview to *Le Monde*, in which he more explicitly revealed his fondness for a specific type of shopping:

I would say (...) that I have an almost obsessive relation to writing instruments. I often switch from one pen to another just for the pleasure of it. I try out new ones. Besides, I have far too many pens — I don't know what to do with all of them. And yet, as soon as I see them, I start craving them. I cannot keep myself from buying them.

When felt-tipped pens first appeared in the stores, I loved them a lot. (The fact that they were originally from Japan was not, I admit, displeasing to me.) Since then I've become tired of them, because the point flattens out too quickly.

I've also used nibs — not the 'Sergeant-Major', which is too dry, but softer nibs, like the 'J'. In short, I've tried everything... except Bics, with which I feel absolutely no affinity. I would even say, a bit nastily, that there is a 'Bic style', which is really just for churning out cheap copy, writing that merely transcribes thoughts.

In the end, I always return to fine ink pens. The essential thing is that they can produce that soft, smooth writing I absolutely hold dear.[7]

Somewhat strangely, perhaps, the interview made no reference whatever to a text entitled 'Variations sur l'écriture' (variations on writing) that Barthes had written earlier that same year. This delightful piece saw Barthes approaching the familiar term 'writing' in a way that differed from the 'metaphorical sense' that he usually preferred (*OC* IV, 267). 'Today', he wrote in the opening paragraph, '(...) it is to the manual sense of the word that I would like to come, it is "scription" (the muscular act of writing, of tracing letters) that interests me' (267). Meanwhile, five years before the love of colour would lead him to buy sixteen bottles of Sennelier ink in one afternoon, Barthes entitled a later section of his text, quite simply, 'Couleur':

To be examined: coloured writings — the few of them that exist. Colour is impulse; we are afraid to sign our messages with it; that is why we write black [*nous écrivons noir*]; we only allow ourselves well-ordered, flatly emblematic exceptions: blue for distinction, red for correction. Any change of colour [*toute saute de couleur*] is particularly incongruous: can you imagine yellow, pink, or even grey missives? Books in red-brown, in forest green, in Indian blue? And yet, who knows if the meaning of the words would not be changed? (302)

'Variations sur l'écriture' remained unpublished in Barthes's lifetime. It made a brief, ghostly appearance on 9 February 1980, however, in the course on the preparation of the novel, when, prompted by a mnemonic that read 'Mon texte sur l'écriture' (my piece on writing), Barthes discussed the relationship between a writer's style, 'obsessive care (...) given to choice of nibs, paper, etc.', and the way in which he or she subsequently formed letters upon the page (*PR*, 339). Proust, for instance, wrote 'at a gallop', and 'all of his work depended upon this muscular ability' (338). 'In a general way', Barthes concluded, 'one could risk defining the work *as a kinetic relationship between head and hand*' (339, emphasis in original).

One final ink blot. *Roland Barthes by Roland Barthes*, which is book-ended (in the French edition, at least) by elegant handwritten statements, reveals the obsessive care with which the narrator constructed his working environments:[8]

> Another *Argo*: I have two work spaces, one in Paris, the other in the country. Between them there is no common object, for nothing is ever carried back and forth. Yet these sites are identical. Why? Because the arrangement of tools (paper, pens, desks, clocks, calendars) is the same: it is the structure of the space which constitutes its identity. This private phenomenon would suffice to shed some light on structuralism: the system prevails over the very being of objects. (*RB*, 46)[9]

Elsewhere, meanwhile, the text incorporates photographs of Barthes surrounded by the materials of writing and painting, and a list of passions that includes 'pens, writing nibs' (*RB*, 116, translation modified). The narrator even manages to reel in a form of ink that had left a smudge upon *Mythologies* almost twenty years earlier: 'I am writing this day after day; it takes, it sets: the cuttlefish produces its ink' (*RB*, 162).[10]

2. Ink: Well?

Why should these 'inkidents' matter? Why are they worth 'inkvestigating'? The interview given to *Le Monde* in 1973 includes an answer to these questions. At first glance, the interviewer's incipit appears to be a little bland: 'Do you', he asks, 'have a method of working?'[11] After giving three brisk sentences in response, however, Barthes turns his attention to the politics of the question itself. There is, he notes, 'a kind of censorship which considers this topic taboo, under the pretext that it would be futile for a writer or an intellectual to talk about his writing, his daily schedule, or his desk' (177). And then, recalling the work of *Mythologies*, he adds:

> When a great many people agree that a problem is insignificant, that usually means it is not. Insignificance is the true locus of significance. This should never be forgotten. That is why it seems so important to me to ask a writer about his writing habits, putting things on the most material level, I would even say the most minimal level possible. This is an anti-mythological action: it contributes to the overturning of that old myth which continues to present language as the instrument of thought, inwardness, passion, or whatever, and consequently presents writing as a simple instrumental practice. (177)

I want to propose that Barthes's many ink blots are the marks of precisely this 'anti-mythological action' at work.[12] Tellingly, the resistance to the myth that makes language an expressive instrument is something that — like the ink blots — colours many of Barthes's texts. *Sade, Fourier, Loyola*, for instance, denounces 'the old modern myth according to which language is merely the docile and *insignificant* instrument for the serious things that occur in the spirit, the heart or the soul'.[13] *A Lover's Discourse*, meanwhile, spurns the advances of what it calls 'the illusion of expressivity' (98), and *Sollers Writer* shines light upon the way in which a text like *H* halts the notion that language is merely 'used to transmit ideas or information' (84).

But what does this have to do with *The Neutral*? On a very simple level, the course repeatedly refers to the materials and materiality of inscription. Almost two months after the accident involving the Sennelier ink, for instance, a short subsection entitled 'Private Rites' moves from a consideration of 'the secret ritual the writer has to follow in order to write (. . .) (fountain pens, places, etc.)' to an anecdote about Kafka, Lederer, 'especially bright blue ink' and 'engraved sheets of hand-made paper' (*N*, 123–4). Meanwhile, shortly after discussing the writing habits of Proust and Swedenborg, Barthes once again records his attachment to his beloved fountain pen (144); this, I presume, is the same pen that he subsequently places at the top of a list of objects that he would be unable to surrender if performing 'an act of self-destitution' (150).[14]

Beyond these niblets, however, I want to propose that *The Neutral* more generally allows the link between ink blots and 'anti-mythological action' to take on a particularly caustic, vivid form. The moment at which things became clear to me — the moment at which the ink of the cuttlefish began to disperse — occurs within minutes of *The Neutral* setting off on its way. At the very beginning of the first session, Barthes works through the routine practicalities, distributes 'a list of the texts whose reading, in various ways, has punctuated the preparation of this course' (*N*, 1), reads four epigraphs, and then settles down to what he calls 'the object of this course, its argument' (6). Moments later comes the following: 'Put another way, according to the perspective of Saussure, to which, on this matter, I remain faithful, the paradigm is the wellspring of meaning; where there is meaning, there is paradigm, and where there is paradigm (opposition), there is meaning' (7). Here, that is to say, preliminaries aside, lies the first proper name of *The Neutral*. And a certain fidelity towards this name is professed.

Although the *Course in General Linguistics* does not appear upon the list of formative texts that Barthes has just distributed to his audience, I want to propose that it is penned there in invisible ink. Ink, in fact, is the link, for, minutes after recounting the tale of the spilled Sennelier 'Neutral' on 11 March 1978, Barthes makes an explicit pledge of allegiance: 'I am "Saussurian" = not a "faith" but a willingness to have recourse to (*recourir à*) Saussurian models in order "to understand" [to speak].'(54)[15] What if this article of faith flowed from the spillage that has just been announced? What if Barthes were Saussurian in his repeated references to the material act and objects of writing?

In the section of the *Course in General Linguistics* entitled 'Linguistic Value', Saussure makes the groundbreaking proposition upon which so much poststructuralist theory has depended: 'Without language, thought is a vague, uncharted nebula. There are no pre-existing ideas, and nothing is distinct before the appearance of language.'[16] The sign, in other words, is the condition of thought, not its instrument, medium, expression, or echo. That, as I see it, is Saussure's real breakthrough, the move that makes a world of difference. It is also, I want to suggest, the theoretical point to which Barthes is faithful when he sets, in the form of an 'anti-mythological' struggle, his interest in the materials and material act of writing against the endoxal, expressive model of language.

To put matters in the vocabulary of *The Neutral*, I read Barthes's ink blots as marks of a commitment to a non-arrogant theory of language. Arrogance, of course, is one of the themes that regularly arises in the course of 1977–8. In fact, it appears as early as the opening session, just moments after Barthes has affirmed his fidelity to Saussure (*N*, 7). A little over three months later, he returns to the topic in much more detail, naming a whole section of the course 'Arrogance':

Under the word 'arrogance', I gather all the (linguistic) 'gestures' that work as discourses of intimidation, of subjection, of domination, of assertion, of haughtiness: that claim the authority, the guarantee of a dogmatic truth or of a demand that doesn't think, that doesn't conceive of the other's desire.

One is assaulted by the arrogance of discourse everywhere there is faith, certitude, will-to-possess, to dominate, be it by means of an insistent demand: the inventory of arrogant discourses would be endless, from the political discourse to the advertising discourse, from the discourse of science to that of the 'scene'. We will not draw up this inventory, this typology; it would be more useful to ask under what difficult conditions a discourse manages not to be arrogant (cf. *in fine*, on writing). (152)

I am struck by how the mention of non-arrogance brings close to itself a consideration of writing. Later in the same session of *The Neutral*, in fact, Barthes explicitly pursues this connexion. 'Can writing be arrogant?', he asks in the opening line of a subsection entitled, quite simply, 'Writing' (162). 'My immediate (partial) answer', he continues, 'is: Writing is the very discourse that unfailingly baffles the arrogance of discourse → I have not (or not yet) the conceptual means to theorize this position (that would suppose a "what is writing?").' (162) In the light of 'Variations sur l'écriture', where the final word of the title is given a pluralizing twist, I find the term 'writing' undecidable at this point in *The Neutral*. (The two numbered paragraphs that follow the question 'what is writing?' do not, I feel, settle the matter.) Should it be read as a familiar textual celebration of what *S/Z* calls 'the magic of the signifier', or is it 'the manual sense of the word', to return to the opening page of 'Variations sur l'écriture', that raises its hand here?[17] Might it even, in keeping with the spirit of *The Neutral*, be necessary to hear both possibilities at the same time, to suspend the demand to choose?

I cannot calm these questions with a spilled answer, but I should like to conclude by considering how the 'manual sense of the word' matters, both at this specific moment and elsewhere in *The Neutral*. How might 'the muscular act of writing, of tracing letters' baffle arrogance? How could Barthes's ink blots suspend 'discourses of intimidation, of subjection, of domination, of assertion, of haughtiness'?

The answer lies in the work of Saussure, whose theories, I think, are once again sympathetically penned in invisible ink at the point in *The Neutral* where Barthes asks if writing can be arrogant. The brief discussion that follows the question concludes with an account of the activity of inscription:

The writer: a *Draufgänger* (...) someone carried away, a breakneck, but not arrogant → a drive that generates a stubbornness in practice, not in conviction, in idea: to believe in the importance of what one writes, not of what one thinks → therefore: not loyalty to the idea, but persistence of a practice = what the writer calls 'working' (in his intransitive use of the verb): word of every writer = the last word of Michelet at Hyères before dying: *Laboremus* (no mystique of work ≠ lucid submission to the persistence of language). (*N*, 162–3)

In the emphasis upon 'the importance of what one writes, not of what one thinks', and in the subsequent outlawing of 'loyalty to the idea', I see an inkling of Saussure's challenge to the idealism of the traditional, referential model of meaning. And I read that very challenge — in which the sign is neither expressive nor in the service of the individual — as a glancing blow to a remarkably *arrogant* account of language. If the sign, as common sense would have it, is merely a secondary expression of a preceding idea, then the human being dominates language, brings it close and directs it according to his or her prior intentions. Thought precedes, and it proceeds as the great dictator. It is precisely this arrogance, this 'will-to-possess', that Saussure's theory of language calls into question. And Barthes's ink blots, it seems to me, accomplish precisely the same thing. Their 'antimythological action' is their suspension of an anthropocentric, arrogant account of meaning. By repeatedly writing about the sheer materiality of writing, Barthes signs a commitment to Saussure that works against *doxa*. The 'almost obsessive relation to writing instruments', that is to say, sedates the arrogance of idealism, and it is for this very reason that Barthes's ink blots deserve detailed attention. To ignore them, to wipe them away with a sweeping hand that longs for a pristine page, is to miss a movement against myth.

3. Plumes

There is, of course, a risk. An obsessive interest in the habits of writing could easily be smudged into a fascination with the private lives of Authors that claims to reveal the overflowing individuals who stand behind and before the words on the page. I cannot think of anything more tedious, but I am also aware that I am writing and walking the finest of lines. Biography is a magnet for mediocrity. Its presence in literary studies is a curse that curdles the discipline into vacuous self-satisfaction. Donna Haraway once remarked that 'teaching modern Christian creationism should be fought as a form of child abuse', and I feel the same about the fostering of biography-based criticism.[18] In writing lives, biographers write the obituary of textuality. I am not interested in ink blots if they are taken to honour an Author who has nourished a work. For me, rather, they underscore how inscription cannot be reduced to expression, the transmission of an aching emotion, the sacred sharing of an inner self. Myth drowns in ink.

This is not merely a question of theory. As the pen moves across the page before my eyes, as the ink wells and takes, blood is being spilled around the world for a flash of fundamentalisms that fatally believe the Word to be an expression of the truth of a prophet, a president, a party, or a God. Ink burns at its root, and Barthes's ink blots are spills for a work of fire that glows with the desire for the Neutral.[19]

NOTES

1 Roland Barthes, 'Variations sur l'écriture' in *Œuvres complètes*, edited by Eric Marty, 5 vols. (Paris, Seuil, 2002). Page references follow the abbreviation OC and are included in the text. All translations from this text are my own.
2 Roland Barthes, *La Préparation du roman I & II*, edited by Nathalie Léger (Paris, Seuil/IMEC, 2003). Page references follow the abbreviation PR and are included in the text. All translations from this text are my own.
3 Karl Marx, 'The Eighteenth Brumaire of Louis Bonaparte' in *Surveys from Exile: Political Writings, Volume 2*, edited by David Fernbach (Harmondsworth, Penguin, 1973), 46. Barthes records an obsession with Marx's proposition in *The Neutral*, edited by Thomas Clerc and translated by Rosalind E. Krauss and Denis Hollier (New York, Columbia University Press, 2005), 80–1 and in *Roland Barthes by Roland Barthes*, translated by Richard Howard (Berkeley, University of California Press, 1977), 88 (further page references follow the abbreviations N and RB respectively and are included in the text). Meanwhile, his book on Sollers adds a twist: 'History repeats itself, without doubt, but it must be repeated: *as a spiral*.' *Sollers Writer*, translated by Philip Thody (London, Athlone Press, 1987), 93. Emphasis in original; translation modified.
4 At the risk of being seen as an inkhornist, I have slightly modified the translation here. For the original French wording, see *Le Neutre*, edited by Thomas Clerc (Paris, Seuil/IMEC, 2002), 80–1. The printed version of the course does not record two things that can be heard at this point in the audio recording of the session of 11 March 1978: the laughter that greets Barthes's revelation about the number of bottles purchased, and an aside in which Barthes further explains his fascination with the names given to inks.
5 Does this partially account for the way in which the same body of work is tattooed with numerous references to Gustave Flaubert's *Bouvard and Pécuchet*, translated by Mark Polizzotti (Normal, IL, Dalkey Archive Press, 2005)? Flaubert's text, after all, incorporates its own spillage of ink (246) and revolves around two copyists with excellent handwriting (8–9), one of whom has a name that clearly recalls *un buvard*, the French term for a blotter. So much so, in fact, that the English translation of Barthes's *Fragments d'un discours amoureux* is actually blotted at one point by a reference to 'Buvard and Pécuchet'. Roland Barthes, *A Lover's Discourse: Fragments*, translated by Richard Howard (New York, Hill and Wang, 1978), 199.
6 Roland Barthes, *Empire of Signs*, translated by Richard Howard (New York, Hill and Wang, 1983), 85.
7 Roland Barthes, 'An Almost Obsessive Relation to Writing Instruments' in *The Grain of the Voice: Interviews 1962–1980*, translated by Linda Coverdale (Berkeley, University of California Press, 1991), 178 (translation modified).

8   While the original *Roland Barthes par Roland Barthes* (Paris, Seuil, 1975) features handwritten notices on the inside of the front and back covers, the English translation places the first handwritten image *after* the title page and, more strangely, the first photograph of Barthes's mother. The second example duly comes at the very end of the text, but is not actually printed on the inner face of the back cover.
9   For more on the composition of these workspaces, see 'An Almost Obsessive Relation', 180.
10 For the earlier reference to the cuttlefish and its cloud, see *Mythologies*, edited and translated by Annette Lavers (London, Vintage, 1993), 155.
11 Barthes, 'An Almost Obsessive Relation', 177.
12 Incidentally, I have noticed that one of Barthes's erstwhile students, Antoine Compagnon, also has inky fingers. In writing about reading one of Barthes's manuscripts after his death, Compagnon notes that he is reminded of the body of the absent teacher by the colour of the ink upon the page (Antoine Compagnon, 'Roland Barthes's Novel', translated by Rosalind Krauss, *October* 112 (2005), 25). Could this, I wonder, be called a case of 'inkvoluntary memory' (*mémoire 'encrevolontaire'*)? And is Compagnon sent in search of lost time by the same blue ink in which the notes for *The Neutral*, according to Daria Galateria, were 'illuminated'? (Daria Galateria, 'Les Couleurs du Neutre' in *Roland Barthes: Intermezzo*, edited by Achille Bonito Oliva (Milan, Skira, 2004), 81. Translation is my own.)
13 Roland Barthes, *Sade, Fourier, Loyola*, translated by Richard Miller (Baltimore and London, Johns Hopkins University Press, 1997), 39. Emphasis in original.
14 Barthes does not specify which type of pen he means here – the French text simply refers to 'un stylo' (*N*, 193), as does the audio recording – but I find it hard, given what he says about ballpoints in the interview with *Le Monde*, to believe that it could be anything but a 'stylo plume'. It would seem, moreover, that Barthes's audience on 13 May 1978 (the day on which he spoke of self-destitution and fountain pens) was well aware of his contempt for Bics, for when he announces, near the beginning of the session, that he has just received an anonymous note urging him to retire, there is laughter as soon as he mentions that the letter was written 'with a green ballpoint pen' (*N*, 136). This response is not mentioned in the printed text, but it can be heard on the audio recording.
15 The equals sign and final interpolation in square brackets are in the original text. I have slightly modified the translation here in order to preserve the echo of '*cours*', of what flows, in '*recourir*'.
16 Ferdinand de Saussure, *Course in General Linguistics*, edited by Charles Bally, Albert Sechehaye and Albert Reidlinger, translated by Wade Baskin (London, Fontana, 1974), 112.

17 Roland Barthes, *S/Z*, translated by Richard Miller (New York, Hill and Wang, 1974), 4.
18 Donna J. Haraway, 'A Cyborg Manifesto: Science, Technology, and Socialist-Feminism in the Late Twentieth Century' in *Simians, Cyborgs, and Women: The Reinvention of Nature* (London, Free Association Books, 1991), 152.
19 I should like to thank Laurent Milesi for answering my questions about Barthes's French.

'*Préparation du romanesque*' in Roland Barthes's Reading of *Sarrasine*

ANDY STAFFORD

Abstract:
By considering *S/Z* (1970) as an early example of the *romanesque* (novelistic) in Roland Barthes's *oeuvre*, this article considers the generic and thematic anticipation of *La Préparation du roman* in Barthes's seminars of the late 1960s. It suggests that his seminar notes on Balzac's *Sarrasine* written in 1968 and 1969 (and on which *S/Z* is based) are a form of proto-essayism, albeit given as seminars in the institutional context of the Ecole Pratique des Hautes Etudes in Paris. This essayism is traced through the notion of *perte de soi* (loss of self) evident in two aspects of the seminar notes: firstly, in the 'drugged reading' that Barthes proposes, and then through his ambivalence to the literary character. Working 'retroactively', the article concludes that *La Préparation du roman* can help us to *explain S/Z* and its genesis, that is *proactively*, by applying this *perte de soi* to the act of one about to write a novel.

Keywords: Barthes, *Sarrasine* seminar, 'drugged reading', literary character, depersonalization, loss of self

1. Introduction

In as much as it wishes to establish a link between Roland Barthes's innovative reading of Balzac's short story *Sarrasine* in his seminars in 1968 and 1969, and his final set of lectures, *La Préparation du roman*, ten years later, this article is concerned with the notion of the 'romanesque', rendered into English as 'the novelistic'. Of interest also is the institutional context in which these two examples of Barthes's thought on the *romanesque* appeared, that is the Ecole Pratique des Hautes Etudes (EPHE) in the late sixties and the prestigious Collège de France a decade later. My own research into this institutional question has looked specifically at the EPHE seminars in the late sixties and the *romanesque* in the seminar notes that Barthes wrote for his reading of *Sarrasine* some time around the end of 1967 and the beginning of 1968, which were then given to a postgraduate seminar at the EPHE between February and May 1968 and then November 1968 and April 1969, seminar notes which then became the basis of his 1970 text *S/Z*.[1]

So far I have concentrated on the fact that these seminars were split by the events of May 1968. Indeed, Barthes alludes to May 68 in *La Préparation du roman*, when suggesting that some writers' lives have a historical break in them with a concomitant 'change of sensibility', his being May 68 (*PR*, 362). Therefore we have the first link, retroactively furthermore, between the *Préparation du roman* lectures and *S/Z*. Indeed, proactively (or proleptically), it was of course impossible for Barthes to understand the importance of May 68 in, for example, June 1968; and in that sense 1979 and the *Préparation du roman* lectures could represent, in some small way, a coming to terms with the Events of 1968. So within this change of sensibility between pre- and post-May 68, which Barthes has applied to his own writing, from the vantage point of ten years later, we can see, in intellectual-historical terms, the moves in the late sixties from structural analysis to poststructuralism. This intellectual shift may be a well-proven characterization of the late sixties going into the early seventies period. However, I want to question this rupture for two reasons. Firstly, and Barthes makes this point above, rupture perhaps contains a continuity (poststructuralist elements are evident before May 1968, and structural analyses continue afterwards). Secondly, the rupture and continuity that exist between the seminars on *Sarrasine* and the manuscript of *S/Z* suggest a more important question to answer: how to convert teaching notes into a book — something which the *Préparation du roman* lectures see, of course, only posthumously.

It is, quite naturally, *critique génétique* proper that is most able to look at this passage from teaching notes to published text, and also at that from the *S/Z* manuscript to the final text. However, I want also to consider the notes for the seminars as a 'préparation du Romanesque', in the same spirit as the *Préparation du roman* of ten years later, that is as a potentiality; though realized in book form in his life-time (unlike *La Préparation du roman* for the reason just stated), there is little evidence to suggest that Barthes *knew* in 1968 that his classes and the notes on *Sarrasine* would end up as the book *S/Z*. So there is a sort of *chassé-croisé* here, between 1968 and 1979.

The second link between the seminar notes on *Sarrasine* and the *Préparation du roman* lectures is Barthes's suggested admiration for Balzac's comment that 'hope is a memory which desires': 'Any beautiful or even impressive work functions as a work that is desired, but also as one that is incomplete and even lost *because I did not create it myself*, and which has to be found again by recreating it; to write is to want to rewrite.' (*PR*, 189, italics in original) This idea, and what *La Préparation du roman* calls 'a third term: either the link itself, or the new work, *inspired* by the old one' (*PR*, 192, italics in original), could easily be applied to Barthes's own *œuvre S/Z*, and its relation to Balzac's 'tutor-text'.

Nevertheless, we might consider a comparison of 1968 and 1979 a 'false good suject'.[2] This would be true perhaps were we to use material external to the writings that Barthes's *romanesque* produces. But it is precisely two aspects of his reading of *Sarrasine*, contained in the seminar notes from 1968/69 (only one of which makes it into *S/Z*) that can help us to understand the writerly project of *La Préparation du roman*. It is first the *lecture droguée* and then the consideration of literary character that I want to use to link the reading of *Sarrasine*, in both seminar notes and in *S/Z*, to *La Préparation du roman*. The genetic-generic form of the notes in relation to *S/Z* is central then to *La Préparation du roman*, to what Barthes calls the 'lecture-book'. As an example of 'life-writing' dovetailing with an academic interest in literary texts, the 'lecture-book' will become a key element in *La Préparation du roman*, but one that is 'prepared' by the 'romanesque' way in which he had written his seminar notes on *Sarrasine* and then converted these into the essay *S/Z*.

This meeting of text and life in an institutional setting is best summarized as one of loss, or effacement of self. Both his writing on the literary character in relation to literature in general and to *Sarrasine* in particular, and the idea of 'drugged reading' seem to prepare us for the notion of a *perte de soi*, a loss of self, or desire for the loss of self. It is a notion that seems to characterize the period between *S/Z* and *La Préparation du roman* and that is a distinct strategy in the writing of *Roland Barthes by Roland Barthes* (1975) and *A Lover's Discourse* (1977) in particular; it is also detectable in *Empire of Signs* (1970), in *The Pleasure of the Text* (1973) and even in *Camera Lucida* (1980). Unlike the perverse notion of *perte* one might find in the work of Georges Bataille, and more active than the 'happy' *fading* that both *S/Z* and *A Lover's Discourse* find in textual *aphanisis*, this Barthesian *perte* is a deeply human, if not 'humanist' one, for it seeks to counter the human alienation caused by the desire to 'possess' the Other (by pigeon-holing them), by the self finding itself 'solidifying' under the weight of a whole and centered 'character', by that 'image' of the writer 'earned' by a critic working in the (highly orthodox) field of literary criticism in France.

2. Perte I: Drugged Reading

'Step by step', is, we will remember, the slowed-down method of reading a text advocated in *S/Z* (see digression VI), and which is germane to the cinematographic action of slowing the film to analyse stills.[3] Excised from the final version — though Barthes does talk about re-reading the text 'as though under the effect of a drug' (digression IX) — is any specific reference in *S/Z* to a *lecture droguée*, and to its role in 'slowing-down' the text. Yet in the seminar notes on *Sarrasine* the *lecture droguée* has equal place alongside, is even linked intricately, to the 'step by step' of slowed-down reading, as the following section of the notes shows:

> Step by step: the ideal movement for reading (there is a prejudice that reading is jumping, omitting). The ideal = reading without residue, without omission, pure: a reading made up of acuity, precision, division and perspective: cf. a state that is not dream-like but an hallucination: to read is not to dream (and even less to day-dream), it is to hallucinate, to take a drug (with the idea of hyper-precision that this word has in Baudelaire): Step-by-step: a mode of hyper-aesthetics: drugged reading: erethism in reading (≠ drugged reading), impatience to deflower: the Don Juan approach to reading: do not start again that which has been read once (...): what I have called a drugged reading obviously cannot be explained by any *phenomenology* of reading, as this type of reading assumes *that we do not know where the subject is*: in any case, he is no longer in an armchair.[4]

As we can see from this, an important intertext for the reading of *Sarrasine* and pretext for *S/Z* is Charles Baudelaire's set of essays *Les Paradis artificiels*.[5] However, it is my suggestion that, in citing the 'hyper-aesthetics' that Baudelaire experiences with haschisch and opium, Barthes also takes up a position with regard to drugs that is diametrically opposed to Baudelaire's (and, as we shall see, to Balzac's).

The 'greenish-yellow pomade' (*AP*, 27) that Baudelaire himself takes and its effects on a range of people whose experiences he narrates leave him decidedly unimpressed. Despite the sharpening of the senses occurring under both drugs, it is especially haschisch that alters nothing, Baudelaire suggested: drugs heighten acutely our feelings and thoughts (Barthes's word 'hyper-aesthetics' is his own, it would seem) but no more than that. Haschisch is not simply 'impure', more importantly for Baudelaire it 'is much more devastating than opium' and 'altogether more disturbing' (*AP*, 69–70). Baudelaire describes seeing Balzac refusing to partake in drugs and criticizing them for their encouragement of 'abdication' (88–9); as a good Balzacian, Baudelaire is acutely aware that haschisch tends to disarm the will—and here we begin to see the opposing position that Barthes is taking in his proposed method of reading Balzac. However, by alluding to the hyper-aesthetic of a *lecture droguée*, Barthes seems to be placing himself, the reader (if only metaphorically), precisely where Baudelaire does not want to be. The 'decentering' of self (author, text and reader in particular) that is so characteristic of *S/Z*, as poststructuralist as it is Buddhist, seems well summarized in Baudelaire's (negative) analysis of what happens with haschisch: 'Sometimes a loss of ego occurs (...), the contemplation of the outside makes you forget your own existence. (...) You feel yourself evaporating and you attribute to your pipe the strange power of smoking you' (*AP*, 52–3).

Another intertext, from the early 1960s, is Henri Michaux's 'Lectures sous haschisch'.[6] However, I want to argue that the metaphorical 'drugged reading' that Barthes is invoking in 1968 is prized not so much for the perspicacity to which Michaux alludes, but for its positioning of the self as reader. If it is a loss of self that Baudelaire regrets in *Les Paradis artificiels*, then this is exactly what Barthes is looking for in his reading of *Sarrasine*. Despite the acceleration Baudelaire sees in the effects of haschisch, he is aware also of its slowing-down, rhythmic aspect that destroys reasoning, its 'rhapsodic' train of thought also being 'storm-tossed (...), infinitely more accelerated and more chaotic' (*AP*, 69). This accelerated, but rhapsodied, 'abdication' seems to summarize then *precisely* what Barthes is looking for in the *lecture droguée*, as the musical sensitivity becomes crucial for the destruction of reasoning in the *S/Z* approach to *Sarrasine*.

Not only does the 'stereophonic' nature of competing meanings mark the act of reading in *S/Z*, but also Barthes's reading is deeply idiosyncratic. The division of the units of meaning in *S/Z* treats some of the sentences in *Sarrasine* so quickly so as to *ignore* a hermeneutic and experiential (or closed), centered reading of the Balzac story; the 'reading' itself is contradictory enough to enrage the *belle-lettriste*, scientistic sensibilities of Thomas Pavel and Claude Bremond, to the extent that they completely overlook the profoundly essayistic, even literary nature of *S/Z*.[7] We will return to the question of essayism in the conclusion; first we must establish a link between the *lecture droguée* and a second manner of dissolving the self.

In his lectures on the Neutral of 1977/78, Barthes returns to Baudelaire's treatise on 'artificial paradises' when he discusses the 'naturel excessif' of consciousness that Baudelaire sees drugs producing

(*N*, 95ff.).⁸ As an example of the 'neutral' the 'total sensibility' brought about by drug-taking is then specifically related to a loss of persona: 'one becomes everything, one is no longer anything' (*N*, 99). Thus, with this good example of the *perte* under discussion here, we have a stepping-stone between the *Sarrasine* notes and *La Préparation du roman*. But before we look at the importance of 'disarming' in *La Préparation du roman* we must consider our second 'perte'.

3. Perte II: Depersonalization

It could be suggested that the *lecture droguée* invoked by Barthes in the seminar notes on *Sarrasine* is merely 'parametric' to the reverie in the Balzac story (just as the pensive narrator at the end of *Sarrasine* reflects the 'suspension' of judgement operated by the reader/rewriter in *S/Z*). But this would be to ignore the distinction that Barthes makes in the notes (as we have seen) between dreaming and hallucinating. It would also be to take away the force of 'deconditioning' — an idea used first by Barthes in relation to Alain Robbe-Grillet in the 1950s — that the *lecture droguée* is operating. If Barthes's idea of a 'deconditioning' of reading (here via a hypothetical late-60s drug-taking) goes back to his 1950s writings on the *nouveau roman*, this conveniently leads me onto the other aspect within the *perte de soi* that I want to illustrate in Barthes's *romanesque*, a loss of self which links the late 1960s to the late 1970s; that is, the central question of characterization and nomination within literary discourse.

Depersonalization, even anonymity, is a key feature of the post-war French novel, especially of the *nouveau roman*, and is an important theme in Alain Robbe-Grillet's famous dismissal of the Balzacian literary character.⁹ We will have good reason to come back to the generic question around the literary-theoretical essay, such as Robbe-Grillet's, in the conclusion. Thus, and so typical of the way Barthesian literary theory often runs parallel to (and occasionally dovetails with) a certain literature of the moment, *S/Z* seems fundamentally concerned with literary 'character'. As Bremond and Pavel insist, the literary character is a central feature of *S/Z*, even to the point that Barthes, they say, distorts its role in the semic code.¹⁰ However, this (so-called) distortion seems to me to be central to Barthes's *romanesque* strategy. Rather than generalize the literary character, which is Nathalie Sarraute's Sartrian solution in her novels, for example, Barthes's strategy in his reading of *Sarrasine* — and we will see how this relates to *La Préparation du Roman* in a moment—is to accept the contradictory status of the literary character and then to exploit this contradiction.[11] Donald Rice and Peter Schofer have pointed to this seeming contradiction in relation to the analysis of name and literary character in *S/Z*; my aim here is to underline its role in Barthes's novelistic presentation of self.[12]

Barthes suggested in *S/Z* that 'what is obsolescent in today's novel is not the novelistic, it is the character' (*S/Z*, 95). Yet he still recognized or accepted, even lamented, the predominance of literary character. In his 'Introduction to Structural Analysis of Narratives' of 1966, he had pointed to the way in which Russian formalists such as Tomachevski and Propp had either considered character as irrelevant or had reduced it to a mere typology, not based on a psychology, but a function of the actions imparted by the story.[13] But there is no story in the world without some kind of character or 'actant', and he added in a footnote: 'If one section of contemporary literature has attacked the "character", it is not in order to destroy it (which is impossible), but to depersonalize it, which is quite different.' (ISAN, 257n45) Even Philippe Sollers's radical, seemingly characterless novel of 1965, *Drame*, Barthes argued, had to accept that the subject of the novel, language, was itself a kind of actant or character.[14] By the time of *S/Z*, four years later, Barthes seemed to have reconverted this stricture into a more nuanced view of the literary character: 'From a critical point of view, (...) it is as wrong to suppress the character as it is to take him off the page in order to turn him into a psychological character (...): characters are types of discourse and, conversely, the discourse is a character like the others.' (*S/Z*, 178–9)

Seymour Chatman sees this as evidence of Barthes 'changing his tune' between 1966 and *S/Z* in 1970; but perhaps we can see this as less of a shift than a dialectical formulation, as other critics have suggested.[15] For it seems, in *S/Z* at least, that character is taken as inevitable, and yet fatally flawed in relation to the real, or rather as contaminating all aspects of discourse. This markedly Barthesian ambivalence towards the literary character, especially across the turbulent 1968 period, is further compounded by Barthes's tempered criticism of the literary proper name in his 1967 piece 'Proust and Names', at the end of which he seemed to suggest that, in the wake of Proust, it may be impossible to be a writer without believing in a 'natural', motivated link between names and essences.[16]

Therefore, rather than naively celebrate, or glibly regret, the homo-nominalizing potential of literature, *S/Z* represents, in poststructuralist fashion, Barthes's *romanesque* strategy of wedging *in between* (or outside) of these two poles; and it is then precisely this tension in his thought, between the apparently 'obsolescent' textual character and its literary inevitability, that (as so often in Barthes) is revisited ten years later in *La Préparation du roman*. This answers, in part perhaps, Scheiber's implicit question as to where the structuralist critique of literary character disappears following *S/Z*.[17] However, by the time of *La Préparation du roman*, the critique of character has become a virtue, an aim, even a utopia: if the fictional person is lost in a double bind, then it is precisely this 'lost' persona that, in a good Barthesian spiral, seems to return in the *Préparation du roman* lectures.

The implication of the self (reader, critic, writer), the inscription, or rather the description, of self (as writer about to write, but also as professor at the Collège de France), are the subject of important sections in *La Préparation du roman*, even before we reach the *séance* called 'Life as Work' (*PR*, 275–96) and before Philippe Hamon's treatment of the subject:[18] 'There is a dialectic particular to literature (with, I think, potential for the future) whereby the subject can be shown like a work of art; art can put itself into the very making of an individual; man is less in opposition to the work if he makes himself into a work.' (*PR*, 229) If what stops Barthes writing his 'novel' in these 1979 lectures is the literary character, then indeed we could call the *Préparation du roman* lecture notes a performance of depersonalization (there is no novel, but there is an acting of a novelist about to write), a stage towards the 'life as literature' as Nietzsche would have wanted, the dissolution of his — Barthes's — life into literature. Of course, dissolving the self is very Barthesian (especially in his fascination for Michelet); Haikus and Zen Buddhism, so important in both *La Préparation du roman* and in *S/Z*, play on the loss of self that both the *koan* and these 17-syllable Japanese poems reflect. But Barthes's Zen is not so much existential (as Albert Camus's is in his *Noces*), as intellectual and writerly: to be a non-novelist in both senses, non-person and to produce no novel. As Barthes puts it in note-form, so succinctly, in *La Préparation du roman*: 'to speak like a book $\neq$ to live as book, as Text' (*PR*, 149).

Thus *La Préparation du roman* is trying to achieve the utopian position whereby not only is character eschewed (there is no novel, only the *romanesque*), but the writer/critic/academic is also effaced. As Barthes wrote in 1966: 'In fact, narration strictly speaking (the code of the narrator), *like language*, knows only two systems of signs: personal and apersonal.' (*ISAN*, 283, my empahsis)

We have seen how depersonalization was conveyed in the late 1960s by an 'impersonalist' *lecture droguée*, in which 'text' was set in opposition by Barthes to a 'scientism' of literature towards which structuralist literary analysis had been edging ever closer; however, this was a generalized reading, albeit slowed to a 'step by step'. It is the addition of the deep ambivalence towards naming and characterization, in a life-into-literature strategy seemingly required by an academic context, which allows Barthes to glimpse a utopian novel, though this is still defined negatively in *La Préparation du roman*.

This negativity is conveyed by Barthes's aim of stopping the 'constant humming' of the writer's *oeuvre* (*PR*, 29). This apersonalism (not simply impersonalism) has an important bearing upon how Barthes writes across the 1970s — what we might call his 'novelistic' period — in that it constantly tugs at the 'solid', even solidified, figure of the self that the mid-1970s Barthes tries to 'neutralize'. Just as the narrator is seen in *S/Z* as a character, so too, one could argue, is the writer in its Barthesian version; except that, and this is the importance of the *romanesque* for the essayist-professor, it is a depersonalized version that Barthes's writing is instrumentalizing: to avoid being the Proper Name which he describes in *S/Z* as 'an adjective, an attribute, a predicate' (190). The Proper Name, the character, may be unavoidable in narrative, but it is precisely this that Barthes, the French intellectual figure, strives to avoid in himself, in his imaginary and in his 'image', and which, in a manner not dissimilar to the North-African superstition towards Photography, wishes to escape the box into which the Other tries to place him, to escape a kind of death.

Interestingly then, in *La Préparation du roman*, Barthes characterizes the dialectical outcome of his lectures in Sartrian terms of 'death', which we could apply easily to his reading (and then rewriting) of *Sarrasine*: 'when I write, and once my writing is finished, the Other stares objectively at my subjectivity, he [sic] denies my freedom: he puts me into the position of one who is dead.' (*PR*, 228) To counteract this 'death', it is a form of loss (*perte* as I have called it) that Barthes actively seeks; hence in *S/Z*, and in *La Préparation du roman*, Barthes must accept the to-ing-and-fro-ing between being radically singular (*S/Z* and *La Préparation du roman* are literally uncopiable performances), and yet producing an image which then could (potentially — though Barthes is careful not to let this happen) ossify him into certain positions. Barthes's sensitivity to naming in *S/Z* — 'to read is to struggle to name' (92) — is being undermined, by the late seventies, by an essayism that refuses to say *his* name, in an essayistic enactment of a famous Lacanian question.[19] Indeed, it is the contradictory nature of the character — a contradiction that Bremond and Pavel either do not see (profoundly), or judge harshly by way of a science of the text — that is important in *S/Z*, and then in *La Préparation du roman*. In other words, the essayistic *perte* of *S/Z* — its provisionality, its contradictory ideas, its 'failure' as method (according to Bremond and Pavel) — is its *romanesque* strength: it signifies the refusal to control, to own, or to finish. The gap between the 'true-to-life' and the 'intelligible' that Scheiber sees as a fundamental tension in Barthes's literary analysis of the referential illusion (in both character and textual 'insignificance') is the same gap that Barthes will open up in trying to undermine his own 'image' (or 'character') that 1970s media-dominated intellectual culture in France is trying to impose.[20] If removing (Balzacian) 'will' from reading is equal to the refusal to write a novel in *La Préparation du roman*, then these final lectures are a writing that is now 'step by step', 'drugged': in abdicating and disarming the novelistic sensibility required to start writing a novel, Barthes is also the ex-nominated novelist of *perte*. We are now in a position then to suggest the generic links between the 1968 reading of *Sarrasine* and the thoughts on preparing an act of novel-writing of ten years later.

4. Conclusion

To conclude, I want to consider the generic nature of the *Sarrasine* seminar notes, genetically as it were: what *are* they? They are perhaps the first example of what Thomas Clerc has hinted at in his preface to *The Neutral*, when he describes these lectures as being given by a 'unique' image in French literature, that of the 'artist-professor' (*N*, xxv). Indeed, Barthes had called his notes and seminars on *Sarrasine*, before their publication in book form in *S/Z* in 1970, a 'lecture-book'; similarly, ten years later in *La Préparation du roman*, he describes the lectures as 'a Book-Lecture' or 'Theatre-Lecture' (*PR*, 229) and talks about, one day, even lecturing on the 'Préparation' of the lecture! (*PR*, 233)

This essayism forms the basis of both his seminar and lecture notes, in 1968 seminar-writing and in 1979 lecture-writing: digressive; provisional in their use of effacement; a challenge to 're-write' Balzac and a discussion of how to write a novel; 'semelfactive' performances (or theatricalization) as forensic experiments, but also generically experimental (seminar or lecture theatre as laboratory): not just 'lecture-book', but somewhere between essay, fiction and experiment, what Barthes calls in *La Préparation du roman*, following the German Romantics, 'motleyness' (*PR*, 202), an inter-generic (or extra-generic) form for which *perte* becomes seemingly indispensable.

What then *is* the difference between *La Préparation du roman* and the 'préparation du romanesque' of my title, and above all when one is a preparation for the other? One could use the deconstructive, intertextual 'turn' of *The Pleasure of the Text* and suggest that the *Préparation du Roman* lectures *anticipate* the 'préparation du romanesque' in *S/Z*; and in one sense, by a ruse of les Editions du Seuil, this is true: we will come to read these *Sarrasine* seminar notes, when they appear in 2008, *via La Préparation du roman*—retroactively if you like, or as a function of the 'late' Barthes being preferred to the 'middle' or 'high' versions. We could also apply an approach that is thoroughly romanticist instead, whereby *La Préparation du roman* and the 'préparation du romanesque' are in parallel (or dialogue): equal, identical in their institutional Foucauldian 'play'. Either way, Barthes's essayism—a fictionalized, provisional and highly digressive form (or 'divagatory', to quote Mallarmé)—informs and launches, in both seminar notes on *Sarrasine* and in *S/Z*, the *romanesque* that is crowned by *La Préparation du roman*.

This essayism, or *romanesque*, is not (or is less) compromised in language than that deployed by a novelist such as Sarraute or Robbe-Grillet, in their switching to use the prose essay to discuss the novel and the new literary sensibility of the postwar period, in the most standard and unproblematic fashion.[21] In this sense, Barthes's 'lecture-books' are far more honest: language is, after all, faulty or deeply ambivalent especially in non-fictional prose concerning fiction; and Barthes's essayism, institutionalized but fully aware of its potentiality as 'text', is also far more productive, in that the relationship between tutor-text and critical-text is not beholden to any scientism, is also parametric to its intertexts, and is even possibly a creative form of criticism.

We can now perhaps suggest a rule-of-thumb for the 'artist-professor' or 'critic-novelist': the essayistic wager that marks Barthes's *écriture* is such that the more 'institutional' or more constrained the context, the more corrosive and provisional the writing that emerges; the more an essayism is beholden to complicity with participants in an academic situation, the more a notion of *perte* is required. As he puts it in *La Préparation du roman*: 'a lecture is, to my mind, a specific production, neither entirely writing, nor completely a speech, and marked by an implicit interlocution (a silent complicity)' (31).

If essayism (at least in Barthes's version of it) and *perte* are crucial components for the 'artist-professor', then the *romanesque* now becomes the risk for Barthes of *not* writing a novel: just as the reading of a Balzac story is easy compared to its rhapsodic, drugged slowing-down in a university seminar room, so writing a novel is 'easy' when compared to discussing its 'preparation' in a Collège-de-France lecture series. However, the *Préparation* lectures do have one fundamental difference from the *Sarrasine* seminar notes: what is crucial, with respect to *S/Z*, is to determine whether these seminar notes that precede it are a simple *avant-texte* crowned by their publication in the essay — and 'romanesque' form — that is *S/Z*; or whether the 'lecture-book' — that is, the institutional status of the rewriting of Balzac — has *increased* the essayistic nature of the enterprise, to which *S/Z* then becomes a (poorer?) testimony? In other words (and this question does now apply equally to *La Préparation du roman*), what is the relationship between teaching, lecturing, seminaring, and the essay, the essayistic, the *romanesque*?

My only answer to this is alas, for the moment, in the form of another question: 'So what is to be done', laments Barthes at the end of *La Préparation du roman*, 'for someone like me who is not fully a writer and who is also not a mere socialite?' (272).

NOTES

1 I am grateful to IMEC for permission to quote parts of Barthes's 'Sarrasine' seminar notes; these notes are the earliest version of *S/Z* (Paris, Seuil, 1970), translated as *S/Z*, by Richard Miller (New York, Hill and Wang, 1974). For the Collège de France lecture course, see Roland Barthes, *La Préparation du roman I & II*, edited by Nathalie Léger (Paris, Seuil/IMEC, 2003). Page references follow the abbreviation *PR* and are included in the text. Translations are my own.

2 In a discussion with Maurice Merleau-Ponty (in 1953 or 1954) about a semiology of clothing (*PR*, 177), the philosopher suggested to Barthes that it was a 'false good subject', an idea reiterated in the seminar notes on *Sarrasine*: 'Clothing: a false fine subject (Merleau-Ponty): seemingly very rich in meanings and yet in the end very hard to say anything about' (IMEC, 'Sarrasine', Chemise 5, 15).

3 See Barthes's piece published the same year as *S/Z*, 'The Third Meaning. Research Notes on Some Eisenstein Stills' (1970), in *A Barthes Reader*, edited by Susan Sontag (New York, Hill and Wang, 1982), 317–33.

4 IMEC, Barthes, 'Sarrasine', Chemise 2, pp. 12–12^2.

5   Charles Baudelaire, *Artificial Paradise* [1860], translated by Patricia Roseberry (Harrogate, Broadwater House, 2000). Page references follow the abbreviation *AP* and are included in the text.
6   In 'Relation G' of *Connaissance par les gouffres* (Paris, Gallimard, 1967 [1961]), 172–5, Michaux writes: 'Reading whilst on haschisch opens up the interior space of the sentences and the hidden preoccupations emerge from it, it pierces them in one go.' (175) Translation is my own.
7   Claude Bremond and Thomas Pavel, *De Barthes à Balzac. Fictions d'un critique, critiques d'une fiction* (Paris, Albin Michel, 1998).
8   Roland Barthes, *The Neutral*, edited by Thomas Clerc and translated by Rosalind E. Krauss and Denis Hollier (New York, Columbia University Press, 2005). Page references follow the abbreviation *N* and are included in the text.
9   See Alain Robbe-Grillet, 'On Several Obsolete Notions' [1957], in *For A New Novel* (New York, Grove Press, 1965), 27–9.
10 See Bremond and Pavel, *De Barthes à Balzac*, 137, 142–3.
11 Sartre's notion of 'generality' of character appears in his introduction to Nathalie Sarraute's *Portrait d'un inconnu* (Paris, Gallimard, 1956 [1948]), 10.
12 For the 'double synecdochal role' of the name in *S/Z*, see Rice and Schofer, '*S/Z*: Rhetoric and Open Reading', in *L'Esprit créateur* 22:1 (1982), 33n5.
13 Roland Barthes, 'Introduction to the Structural Analysis of Narratives' in *A Barthes Reader*, 251–95. Page references follow the abbreviation *ISAN* and are included in the text.
14 Barthes's 1968 reworked version of his 1965 review of Sollers's novel *Drame*, 'Drame, poème, roman', is useful in tracking his critique of 'character'; see *Tel Quel, Théorie d'ensemble* (Paris, Seuil, 1968), 27–42, especially 'notes' I–III that Barthes adds to his original review.
15 Seymour Chatman, *Story and Discourse: Narrative Structure in Fiction* (Ithaca/London, Cornell University Press, 1978), 115. See the editors' introduction to *Roland Barthes*, edited by Mike Gane and Nicholas Gane (London, Sage, 2004), vol 1, xiv, and Raymond J. Wilson, 'A Map of Terms: The "Cultural Code" and "Ethic Psychology" in *S/Z* and "Introduction to The Structural Analysis of Narratives"' [2000], in *Roland Barthes*, edited by Gane and Gane, vol 2, 329–45.
16 'Proust and Names', republished in Barthes, *New Critical Essays*, translated by Richard Howard (Berkeley, University of California Press, 1990).
17 Andrew J. Scheiber, 'Sign, Seme and the Psychological Character. Some Thoughts on Roland Barthes's *S/Z* and the Novel' [1991], in *Roland Barthes*, edited by Gane and Gane, vol 2, 301–13 (302–3).
18 Philippe Hamon, 'Pour un statut sémiologique du personnage', in R. Barthes, W. Kayser, W. Booth, Ph. Hamon, *Poétique du récit* (Paris, Seuil, 1977), 115–80 (118–19).

19 'Is the subject I speak of when I speak the same as the subject who speaks?', a Lacanian *mot* cited by Barthes in 1966 (*ISAN*, 283n52).
20 Scheiber, 'Sign, Seme and the Psychological Character', 309–10.
21 See, for example, Robbe-Grillet's 'advice' in *For A New Novel* to those readers looking for psychology, socialist moral or religion in the novel: 'The man interested in these disciplines will read essays and risk less' (35).

Preparing the Novel: Spiralling Back

Jonathan Culler

Abstract:
La Préparation du roman, Barthes's course at the Collège de France which was interrupted by his death in 1980, announces a change of life: not giving up analysing literature and culture to write a novel but 'preparing the novel', working as if he were going to write a novel. Barthes's approach to the novel is quite singular. With no interest in narrative, nor in extracting the meaning from experience, he treats the novel as a sort of notation, and perversely takes Haiku as a model. This new project constitutes in many respects a regression to literary and cultural ideas Barthes had previously rejected. Most seriously, it involves a turn away from reflection on language, which had been crucial to Barthes's work. But there are other ways in which the change in approach brings new insights to a thinking of the novel and of literature.

Keywords: novel, metalanguage, Barthes, text, literature, writing

Roland Barthes's final course of lectures, *La Préparation du roman*, makes tantalizing reading, perhaps especially because it was suppressed for a number of years and so has the allure of forbidden fruit. It is especially tantalizing to me: as a great admirer of Barthes's work living in Paris in 1979–1980, I found these lectures about the habits of writers sufficiently irritating that I was very irregular in my attendance, preferring other Parisian intellectual activities of greater substance or theoretical interest — a choice which I of course deeply regretted after Barthes's tragic death cut short the course.

But these contingent reasons aside, *La Préparation du roman* is attractive and seductive because it takes place under the injunction of Rilke's 'you must change your life'. The determination to forge a *vita nova* rather than persevere in an academic routine certainly elicits sympathy and admiration, even if one is tempted to ironize on the form it takes for Barthes — not resigning his chair and heading off for Morocco to write a novel but choosing to give a course at the Collège de France about preparing to write a novel! But Barthes presents it well: 'I have to choose my last life, my new life, Vita Nova' (*PR*, 28).[1] To change his life, escape *acedia*, for him entails finding a new practice of writing. He will organize his life around a single or unique task: not writing a novel but working *as if* he were writing a novel, identifying with the perspective of this consecration of one's life to the fantasy of the novel.

This is a paradoxical operation: teaching a course about preparing to write a novel. Imagining this novel, Barthes espouses what he calls the desire to write (*vouloir-écrire*) and tells us straight away that 'writing is not fully writing unless there is a renunciation of metalanguage. One cannot articulate the desire to write except in the language of writing.' (*PR*, 33) The determination to renounce metalanguage is central to this attempt to change perspective and to write not as a critic or theorist, offering metalinguistic categories to describe the literary objects one studies, but to write from the perspective of the writer preparing the novel. Writing about the desire to write *can be* an eminently novelistic operation, as Proust shows, and perhaps this is why Barthes may be able to imagine renouncing metalanguage in a course *about* preparing to write a novel, but insofar as the course is interesting and effective, it does function as metalanguage: about writing, about novels, about novelistic desire. Proust's *In Search of Lost Time* itself elaborates critical metalanguages, about metaphor, about writing and memory; it is a novel about the novel, which is doubtless part of its great attraction for Barthes, who admits often preferring writer's reflections about writing to the novels themselves. One might imagine that such a *méta-roman* would be the best of both worlds, Barthes's fantasized form, but he resolutely rejects the idea of a novel about the novel (*PR*, 37).

Thus in this course we are from the outset in the domain of paradox or aporia. But this is typical of Barthes. He may mock the metalinguistic but always installs himself in it, playfully, even exuberantly, if reluctantly. He enjoys multiplying metalinguistic categories but without making serious claims for them; he wishes that they were just writing rather than also metalanguage. 'I have a disease: I *see* language', he notes (*RB*, 161).[2] Unable to treat it as transparent, he talks about it, and despite his desire to renounce metalanguage, his malady may be incurable. The metalinguistic is inescapable with him, but he does what he can, after his early years of a euphoria of scientificity, to destabilize his metalanguages. He is given, for instance, to what I call disposable typologies: lists of types of x, which provide insight but are sufficiently idiosyncratic or ludic that we are not likely to preserve them as a framework for future thinking, as a contribution to the metalanguage about fiction, or whatever.

In *Roland Barthes by Roland Barthes*, he speaks of the conceptual oppositions that structure his writing, such as denotation/connotation, readerly/writerly, *écrivain/écrivant*, not as a metalanguage of semiotics or poetics but as devices to generate a text. He borrows from different disciplines, he says,

> certain conceptual procedures, an energy of classification: one steals a language, though without wishing to apply it to the end: impossible to say: this is denotation, this connotation, or: this passage is readerly, this writerly, etc. The opposition is *struck* (like a coin), but one does not seek to *honor* it. Then what good is it? Quite simply, it serves to say something... It is a way to make the text go. (*RB*, 92, italics in original)

La Préparation du roman offers quite a few off-the-cuff typologies: 'a historical typology of ways of writing the "I"' (*PR*, 229), or various typologies of types of writers, a typology based on the distinction between Book and Album, and so on. These are responsible for much of the interest of the course, for me — one of Barthes's great achievements is the discovery of the heuristic force of systematicity, even when the system is not taken seriously. But there is also something winning in the self-exposure of Barthes's desire to be a writer, as if writing a novel were such an extraordinarily difficult feat that the most one can imagine is aspiring to it. His fantasizing of the novel is an especially perverse desire, for he does not want to write his life or to tell a story. His is a fantasy of the *novel* but not of narrative nor of memory, summation, capturing of the past, in the manner of *In Search of Lost Time*, nor certainly of extracting the meaning of experience by casting it in narrative form. What he desires is the possibility of '*une épigraphie personnelle de l'instant*', a writing of the instant, a kind of notation, which he sees as neutral, non-interpretive.

It is this odd conception of the novel that leads him, perversely, to approach it through Haiku, as an art of notation. The fact that Haiku is not a Western form makes it easier to imagine it as a form that resists the Western impulse to interpret — to interpret experience, and to interpret the poem: 'tremendous conditioning in the West to give to any reported fact the alibi of an interpretation', he writes (*PR*, 153). Haiku allegedly seizes the moment, but without a point.

The goal Barthes evokes is that of *une œuvre blanche*, colourless, neutral, silent, stripped-down writing, what he calls, in concluding the course, 'this degree zero of the work' (*PR*, 378), evoking his first book, *Writing Degree Zero*, which described 'colourless writing' not subjected to ordering hierarchies of usage (*WDZ*, 76).[3] Camus's

The Stranger is cited as an example: 'the way a certain silence has of existing' (*WDZ*, 78). But Camus' novel, once seen as neutral notation, now seems a distinctive style of literature, and the early Barthes understood this mechanism very well. 'Nothing is more fickle than a colourless writing', for writing that strives to be neutral, undefined, 'un-literary', nevertheless becomes *une écriture*, a way of connoting literature, 'which appears afresh in lieu of an indefinite language'; mechanical habits develop where freedom existed (78). This, I would say, is a semiotic law: neutralization becomes a style and signifies. Thus, the avoidance of meaning or logic becomes, for instance, the theatre of the absurd and signifies powerfully. The early Barthes, shrewd analyst of signifying mechanisms that he was, understood this. Then, while imagining a utopia of language, he recognized the impossibility of escaping literature; thus there is, in *Writing Degree Zero*, 'un tragique de l'écriture', writing as a form of the tragic.

La Préparation du roman seems to resolve this problem by *not* moving to execution, by only *imagining* writing the desired work, so that there can be no disappointment with language hardened into style, manner, and a way of being literature. But it also seems true that Barthes's understanding of the *degré zéro* is quite different nearly 30 years later. 'The desired work', he writes, 'should be simple, filial, desirable' — a surprising trinity (*PR*, 378).

Simple. For *La Préparation du roman*, the work is simple in its 'submission to an aesthetics of the readerly', which Barthes stresses involves (1) 'an overall narrative or logico-intellectual structure', (2) 'a non-deceptive anaphoric system', (3) a renunciation of metalanguage and (4) a renunciation also of irony, pastiche, quotation marks (376–7). Thus Blanchot, who figures in *Writing Degree Zero* as an instance of *le tragique de l'écriture* is in *La Préparation du roman* explicitly disavowed: 'admirable theorist (even if my project rejects his) of this kind of disappointment, of the tragic extenuation of literature' but one for whom the work 'can no longer be anything but what I have to say about it' (380).

Filial. The *œuvre desireé* is continuous with tradition, not based on rupture. It is a matter, Barthes writes, 'of recourse to a kind of heredity of noble values' (381). This is surprising, given Barthes's commitment in *Writing Degree Zero* and elsewhere to writing practices that attempt to refuse literariness, outplay language and disrupt the conventions of prior *écritures*, especially those linked to *valeurs nobles*.

Finally, *desirable*. The work should be the embodiment of desire of or for language, especially French, linked not to the disruptive pleasure of *jouissance*, which *The Pleasure of the Text* had promoted as the supreme value, but to the aesthetic: 'the aesthetic, not to be abandoned', he writes, 'a category that is conceived or conceded by society as a guarantee of noble desire' (383). Raymond Picard, who attacked Barthes's cynical psychoanalytic reading of Racine, would doubtless feel vindicated.[4]

This account of the *œuvre desirée* certainly reverses values previously articulated and adopts views previously combated. S/Z begins with an evaluation linked to a practice of writing: a distinction between 'what it is possible to write, and on the other, what it is no longer possible to write' (*le lisible* or the readerly). The writerly is our value, he declares. Why? 'Because the goal of literary work (or literature as work) is to make the reader no longer a consumer but a producer of the text.'[5] In this value scheme, the readerly is the negative, the *contravaleur*: a value of consumption rather than writing.

One could multiply examples of the renunciation of previously articulated analytical perspectives and the embrace of what had previously been rejected as bourgeois. Along with the embrace of the readerly, the most striking are the revival of the *author* and celebration of the *œuvre* by one who had proclaimed the death of the author and embraced the movement of modern thought leading away 'from work to text', as his famous essay put it.[6] It could be a familiar story: the old man renouncing the radical thought of his youth to embrace the values he had previously contested. In the political realm, aging leftists do often embrace the right, but it seldom happens so explicitly in literature: Robbe-Grillet does not come to write like Balzac; the aging Mallarmé doesn't belatedly decide to imitate Victor Hugo.

Barthes himself deploys the figure of the spiral to describe his movement. Under *Filiation*, he writes, 'accept the aristocracy of writing → I return to Mallarmé's conception of the *Livre* (don't say that I am deploying a slogan that is a century old; this slogan had disappeared for a century; it is a matter of making it return in another place, *en spirale*)' (381). But if a hundred year's absence helps to justify the figure of the spiral, what about the return to the author, to the *œuvre* and the *lisible*, which had scarcely disappeared, though they had been contested by Barthes? In some cases the figure of the spiral is linked to something like a dialectical movement of thought. Concerning the choice of forms, he writes that content, set aside, returns *en spirale* as the implication of form, 'the responsibility of form' (*PR*, 255). A more dramatic example concerns interpretation: the literal, the resistance to interpretation returns *en spirale*. 'The failure of interpretation — interpretability (defying interpretation) of haiku (or Wu-shi) is not a naiveté, it is a third turn of the screw given to language.' (*PR*, 126) The first moment is that of *bêtise* (stupidity), anti-intellectual tautology, 'un sou est un sou'; the second moment is that of interpretation, where the natural, the non-signifying is transcended; but the third moment is where the natural, the literal returns *en spirale*: 'third moment, that of the naturalness of Wu-shi, of haiku' (126). But how can one tell whether the return *en spirale* is super-sophisticated or self-deluded, a myth?

The essay 'From Work to Text', which summed up a whole series of developments in literary theory and criticism, opposed the traditional conception of the literary work to the modern conception of the text. Barthes spoke of this as 'a change in our idea of language and consequently of the (literary) work' (*FWT*, 56). What makes something text is its force of subversion with regard to the old classifications. Text is what is situated at the limit of the rules of speech-acts (rationality, readability, etc.) It is irreducibly plural, a practice or play of the signifier generating the deferral of the signified. The *œuvre*, Barthes wrote then, is 'enmeshed in a process of filiation' (note this term that comes back), and there is appropriation of the work to its author, the father and proprietor.' The work is sacralized, while text is transgressive. The pleasure of the work is 'a pleasure of consumption', unlike the active hedonistic play to which the text invites (*FWT*, 61–2).

In *La Préparation du roman* Barthes explicitly adopts the sacralization of the work and shows no interest in text any more. One could certainly argue that 'From Work to Text' fetishized the idea of text — so much so that there were no actual texts to be found and the most that one could say was that *il y a du Texte*, some Text, in the most interesting works. But in the course we have reversion to the Work as the fetishized object of desire — only the desire of the would-be writer rather than the critic, the Work as fantasized totality — with no reason to think that we are spiralling back to it at another level rather than embracing something once rejected. I note that the interest in language, which animated the earlier conception — a change in our idea of language and consequently of the literary — has simply dropped out rather than been revised in some newly sophisticated way.

As for the author, Barthes's interest is perhaps not so surprising, given his growing pleasure through the years in writing about his own daily habits, his note cards, his desk and so on. But the viewpoint adopted in the course does suspiciously recall the fetishization of authors as geniuses who produce *œuvres*—a concept that he had worked to destroy in the most influential phase of his critical and theoretical career. In *La Préparation du roman* he cites his article 'The Death of the Author' as example of the tendancy to 'erase the author to the benefit of the Text as a structure transcendent with respect to the author', adding 'today I take a completely opposite view' (*je suis aux antipodes de cette attitude*) (276), but his attempt to defend the return as more sophisticated is unconvincing. He writes, 'Telegraphically: Death, lack of curiosity (*incuriosité*), return of curiosity, return of the author', as if the Death of the Author were not a theoretical position but just a lack of curiosity about authors (276).

In the article of *Mythologies* called 'The Writer on Holiday', Barthes had satirized the media's interest in the life of the writer, and concluded that the details of the writer's daily life, far from bringing one closer to the nature of his inspiration and making it clearer, actually emphasize the mythical singularity of his condition.[7] And there are moments in *La Préparation du roman* when he does show signs of a continuing critical attitude towards the myth of the writer. In Castex and Surer, the scholastic manual which embodies the *idées reçues* that Barthes had combated, he finds 'one thing that is surprising and amusing in its regularity, a real tic: the life of practically every author is articulated by a central crisis, from which flows a renewal of the work, that is, from which the triumphant Œuvre arises' (*PR*, 326). Noting that the idea of crisis is facile and attuned to the needs of the myth of the productive crisis (*crise féconde*), he nevertheless uses Castex and Surer's manual, 'which is at once completely mythical but well done' to produce a typology of crises (anecdotal, amorous, political, spiritual) that is hard to differentiate from Barthes's other typologies (327). Indeed earlier in the course he declares, 'In my story (story of a man who wants to write, to undertake an Œuvre), the idea of the Œuvre, solemnified, is linked to that of a Rupture, a new Way of Life, the Organization of a New Life, Vita Nova', with mythifying capitals on all these nouns (280). It is hard to distinguish Castex and Surer's myth from Barthes's own imaginary here.

To me the most irritating return, a regression rather than a spiral, is the conception of exemption from meaning which had long tempted Barthes. In *Roland Barthes by Roland Barthes* he writes that he dreams of a world which would be exempt from meaning, as one is exempt from military service, and he shrewdly lists forms this dream has taken in his work. When Barthes is analysing literature, he produces compelling accounts of attempts to get beyond meaning by disrupting it (and he is all too aware of the semiotic law by which such effects come to signify in turn), but when he ventures outside literature his dream takes naive forms (perhaps admirable as utopian aspiration but naive as theoretical description). Photographs, in *Camera Lucida*, are claimed simply to present reality directly: in a particular photograph of a slave, 'slavery was given without mediation, the fact was established without method'.[8] Giving himself over to myth, he repeats this with Haiku in the course, as in the reflection cited earlier, which suggests, without argument, that because the claim to exemption from meaning is not tautological it constitutes a third moment rather than a regression. Long ago Barthes's little article 'The Reality Effect' (1968) analysed, correctly, the way in which apparent absence of meaning *signifies* the real rather than simply instantiating it.[9] The older Barthes has never offered an analysis to show why this is wrong or could be transcended.

But despite such regressions, which are dangerous in that they might seduce readers into abandoning Barthes's earlier astute analyses, readers should be capable of ignoring these failures while profiting from new insights that preparing the novel yields. Simulating someone who wants to write an *Œuvre* gives us a different perspective from the usual critical one. First, it removes the element of necessity that so often presides over critical analyses, which characteristically seek to show why things had to be just so and not some other way. It introduces a thinking of multiple possibilities and criteria such as 'finishability' (*la finissabilité*) — what would make it possible to complete the work (*PR*, 261).

Second, Barthes had previously treated *to write* as an intransitive rather than transitive verb:[10] one wants to write, not to write something in particular — writing as a compulsion, a destiny, linked to that undifferentiated object, the text. Here, rethinking the matter from the perspective of *doing*, he recognizes that this view needs qualification: *écrire* as absolute and intransitive is one historical possibility among others, and to write is generally to aim at writing something, organized by a fantasy or a model, as in his own case.

The would-be writer is a hero confronted with three tasks or tests (*épreuves*): *choice*, *patience*, and *separation*. The task of choice is much the most pertinent to knowledge of literature. Focus on the models of the book that a writer might have in mind produces some interesting typologies — the *ur-livre*, *le livre-guide*, *le livre clef* and *l'anti-livre*, for instance (*PR*, 242–9), or the distinction between the *Livre*, with its variants, *le livre total, le livre somme, le livre pur* and the album. But there are other typologies that do not work so well, such as that of roles in the writing of a life, that is, types of 'I'. *Persona* is the everyday empirical individual (*personne civile*); *scriptor* the writer as social role — the image of the writer; *auctor* the 'I' that authorizes the writing (*le je garant de ce qu'il écrit*) and *scribens*, the 'I' that exists only in the practice or play of writing (279–80). Using the term *persona* for the *personne civile* indicates that Barthes has no desire to contribute helpfully to critical metalanguage, in which *persona* has a quite different established meaning, but is happy to sow confusion with these throwaway typologies.

The most fully developed critical discussion from the perspective of writing comes under the heading of *Ça prend*: how all of a sudden the work comes together (*l'œuvre prend*). Well into his thirties, Proust was hesitating between the novel and the essay, but suddenly, we don't know why, in the summer of 1909, everything fell into place, he hit upon a 'third form' that would abolish the contradiction between Novel and Essay through its handling of time and its invention of the narrator who recounts his desire to write. Barthes identifies the four key elements as (1) the discovery of the right proper names, (2) the invention of the right 'I', (3) the shift in proportions, from a small project to a vast one and (4) most important, he believes, the device of recurring characters (*PR*, 330–1). This discussion involves an interesting shift in ways of thinking about the novel in general and Proust in particular: vision from the beginning rather than the end, where the finished work is a given and one analyses the significance of different elements in that context.

Barthes's approach through the desire to write also yields another sort of claim. Focusing on what in the novel attracts him, beside the idea of notation, he conceives of the novel not as a story to be recounted but as moments of truth. Joyce's notion of epiphany is one example, but Barthes finds in the episodes of the death of the narrator's grandmother in Proust's *In Search of Lost Time* and the death of Prince Bolkonsky in Tolstoy's *War and Peace* two 'moments of truth' where suddenly literature coincides with an emotional event for the reader who suffers: 'what in my reading happens to me' (*ce qui dans une lecture m'arrive à moi*) (*PR*, 156). There is compact combination of affects of death and love on the one hand, and on the other 'looming up (*surgissement*) of the uninterpretable' (159). Though pathos is scorned today, one could, Barthes writes, theorize a *critique pathétique*, an account of the novel based on these *moments forts*, powerful 'moments of truth which are its absolute justification' (160). The novel becomes, in this account, 'an interweaving, variegated, motley, embroidered' (*un tissu* poikilos, *bigaré, tacheté, brodê*), a combination of notations and inventions, 'a heterology of the True and the False' (160). This theory of the novel would no longer take plot as the fundamental structure but rather these affective elements or moments.

This conception may begin as the vision of someone preparing to write a novel, but it becomes a significant critical claim about the nature of the novel — one that deserves to be debated. It might, in fact, link up with developments in narratology, such as Monika Fludernik's magisterial *Towards a Natural Narratology*, which claims that 'narrative is narrative not because it tells a story but because the story that is tells is reportable'; it 'renders one's own or another's experience within an evaluative frame'.[11] In respects such as this, *La Préparation du roman*, Barthes admits, will install us 'in a small sector (*un petit canton*) of literary theory' (*PR*, 187).

But finally, there is one respect in which the return of the author deserves the accolade *spirale* rather than regression. Barthes is not interested in the thought of authors, nor concerned with their historical intentions, or social and political situations — factors usually taken as determining in biographical criticism. He prefers, as he says, 'la nébuleuse biographique', the biographically hazy, perhaps, or *biographèmes* — salient images, which are, in fact, novelistic, life as literature (*PR*, 278). What comes back with the return of the author is not the traditional author but, he writes, 'the division, fragmentation, or pulverization of the subject' (279).

So there are significant gains in this return, *en spirale*, of what had previously been rejected. The most eloquent expression of the attractions of the return to traditional literary values came in Barthes's inaugural lecture of 1976, *Leçon*:

The old values are no longer transmitted, no longer circulate, no longer impress; literature is desacralized, institutions are impotent to defend and impose it as the implicit model of the human. It is not, if you will, that literature is destroyed; rather *it is no longer protected*: so this is the moment to go there. Literary semiology is, as it were, that journey that lands us in a country free by default; angels and dragons are no longer there to defend it. Our gaze can fall, not without perversity, upon certain old and lovely things, whose signified is abstract, out of date. It is a moment at once decadent and prophetic, a moment of gentle apocalypse, a historical moment of the greatest possible pleasure. (*IL*, 475–6, italics in original)[12]

But what distinguishes *Leçon* from *La Préparation du roman* is that there it is still a question of semiology and of language, as in this passage:

> But for us, who are neither knights of faith nor supermen, the only remaining alternative is, if I may say so, to cheat with langage, to cheat language. This salutary trickery, this grand imposture which allows us to understand language outside the bounds of power, in the splendor of a permanent revolution of language, I for one call *literature*.
>
> I mean by literature neither a set of works nor a branch of commerce or teaching but the complex graph of the traces of a practice, the practice of writing. Hence, it is essentially the text with which I am concerned — the fabric of signifiers which constitute the work. For the text is the very outcropping of language, and it is within language that language must be fought, led astray — not by the message of which it is the instrument but by the play of words of which it is the theater (...) The forces of freedom which are in literature depend (...) on the labor of displacement he [the writer] brings to bear upon the language. (*IL*, 462, translation modified)

In *La Préparation du roman*, language, the sense that engagement with language is what is crucial, has dropped out and Barthes now seems to want to champion literature, *l'œuvre*, against *texte*. I cannot avoid the conviction that this loss vitiates his last thinking of literature, despite its many attractions and advances.

NOTES

1. Roland Barthes, *La Préparation du roman I & II*, edited by Nathalie Léger (Paris, Seuil/IMEC, 2003). Page references follow the abbreviation *PR* and are included in the text. Translations are my own.
2. Roland Barthes, *Roland Barthes by Roland Barthes*, translated by Richard Howard (New York, Hill and Wang, 1977). Page references follow the abbreviation *RB* and are included in the text.
3. Roland Barthes, *Writing Degree Zero*, translated by Annette Lavers (New York, Hill and Wang, 1968). Page references follow the abbreviation *WDZ* and are included in the text.
4. See Jonathan Culler, *Barthes, A Very Short Introduction* (Oxford, Oxford University Press, 2002), 49–56.
5. Roland Barthes, *S/Z,* translated by Richard Miller (New York, Hill and Wang, 1974), 4.
6. See Roland Barthes, 'From Work to Text' in *The Rustle of Language*, translated by Richard Howard (Berkeley, University of California Press, 1986), 56–64. Page references follow the abbreviation *FWT* and are included in the text.

7 See Roland Barthes, *Mythologies*, selected and translated by Annette Lavers (London, Granada, 1982), 29–31.
8 Roland Barthes, *Camera Lucida: Reflections on Photography*, translated by Richard Howard (New York, Hill and Wang, 1981), 80.
9 See Roland Barthes, 'The Reality Effect' in *The Rustle of Language*, 141–8.
10 See Roland Barthes, 'To Write: An Intransitive Verb?' in *The Rustle of Language*, 11–21.
11 Monika Fludernik, *Towards a Natural Narratology* (London, Routledge, 1996), 70, 318.
12 Roland Barthes, 'Inaugural Lecture, Collège de France' in *A Barthes Reader*, edited by Susan Sontag (New York, Hill and Wang, 1982), 457–78. Page references follow the abbreviation *IL* and are included in the text.

Notes on Contributors

Neil Badmington is Senior Lecturer in Cultural Criticism and English Literature at Cardiff University. He is the author of *Alien Chic: Posthumanism and the Other Within* (Routledge, 2004) and editor of *Posthumanism* (Palgrave, 2000). He is currently working on a book entitled *Hitchcock's Magic*.

Jonathan Culler is Class of 1916 Professor of English and Comparative Literature at Cornell University. He has published numerous works of literary theory: *Structuralist Poetics* (Routledge, 1975), *Saussure* (Fontana, 1976), *The Pursuit of Signs* (Routledge, 1981), *On Deconstruction* (Cornell University Press, 1982), *Barthes* (Fontana, 1983), *Framing the Sign* (Blackwell, 1988), *Literary Theory: A Very Short Introduction* (Oxford University Press, 1997) and most recently, *The Literary in Theory* (Stanford University Press, 2006). An augmented edition of his book on Barthes has been published as *Roland Barthes: A Very Short Introduction* (Oxford University Press, 2002).

Sabine Hillen teaches contemporary French literature and the culture of modernity at the University of Antwerp and is working on a research project at the Jan Van Eyckacademie in Maastricht. An essay on the absence of dialogue in Henry de Montherlant's novels was published by *Les Lettres modernes* as *Le Roman monologue: Montherlant, auteur, narrateur, acteur* (2002); her second book, *Ecarts de la modernité: Le roman français de Sartre à Houellebecq*, will be published shortly by the same publisher. Currently her main interests focus on the sociology of literature and 'nobrow' art and culture.

Diana Knight is Professor of French at the University of Nottingham. She is the author of *Flaubert's Characters: The Language of Illusion* (Cambridge University Press, 1985), *Barthes and Utopia: Space, Travel, Writing* (Clarendon Press, 1997) and *Balzac and the Model of Painting: Artist Stories in 'La Comédie humaine'* (Legenda, 2007). She has edited *Feminism* (*Paragraph*, 1986), *Women and Representation* (with Judith Still, WIF, 1995), *Roland Barthes* (*Nottingham French Studies*, 1997) and *Critical Essays on Roland Barthes* (G. K. Hall, 2000).

Jean-Jacques Lecercle is Professor of English at the University of Paris X (Nanterre). He is the author of *The Violence of Language*

(Routledge, 1990), *Philosophy of Nonsense* (Routledge, 1994), *Interpretation As Pragmatics* (Macmillan, 1999), *Deleuze and Language* (Macmillan, 2002), *L'Emprise des signes: Débat sur l'expérience littéraire* (with Ronald Shusterman, Seuil, 2002), *The Force of Language* (with Denise Riley, Macmillan, 2004) and *A Marxist Philosophy of Language* (Brill, 2006).

Lucy O'Meara is completing a PhD at the University of Nottingham on Roland Barthes's lecture courses at the Collège de France. Her publications include articles on Barthes and on Susan Sontag.

Jürgen Pieters teaches literary theory at Ghent University. He is the author of *Moments of Negotiation: The New Historicism of Stephen Greenblatt* (Amsterdam University Press, 2001) and *Speaking with the Dead: Explorations in Literature and History* (Edinburgh University Press, 2005). *Cultural Histories: An Introduction* (Edinburgh University Press, co-written with Alexander Roose) is forthcoming.

Kris Pint teaches cultural and literary theory at the Department of Architecture and Fine Arts of the Provinciale Hogeschool Limburg. He has recently completed his doctoral thesis on Roland Barthes's 'fantasmatic' semiology, entitled *The Perverse Art of Reading*.

Maarten De Pourcq is a research and teaching assistant at the Katholieke Universiteit Leuven, where he studied Classics and Literary Studies. He is currently preparing a doctoral thesis on Roland Barthes and Greek desire. He has published several articles and essays on the reception of Greek tragedy, Roland Barthes, contemporary performance and Dutch poetry.

Andy Stafford is the author of *Roland Barthes, Phenomenon and Myth. An Intellectual Biography* (Edinburgh University Press, 1998), and co-editor of Barthes's seminar notes from 1968 to 1969 on Balzac's *Sarrasine* (with Claude Coste, Seuil, 2007). He has recently co-edited an anthology of studies of the modern essay in French (with Charles Forsdick, Peter Lang, 2005), contributing a chapter on the photo-essay, and is currently working on a book-length study of photo-texts in French. He is a member of the editorial board of *Francophone Postcolonial Studies* and is Senior Lecturer in French and Francophone Studies at the University of Leeds.